THE HABITS OF LEGALITY

STUDIES IN CRIME AND PUBLIC POLICY
Michael Tonry and Norval Morris, *General Editors*

THE HABITS OF LEGALITY

Criminal Justice and the Rule of Law

Francis A. Allen

New York   Oxford
OXFORD UNIVERSITY PRESS
1996

Oxford University Press

Oxford   New York
Athens   Auckland   Bangkok   Bombay
Calcutta   Cape Town   Dar es Salaam   Delhi
Florence   Hong Kong   Istanbul   Karachi
Kuala Lumpur   Madras   Madrid   Melbourne
Mexico City   Nairobi   Paris   Singapore
Taipei   Tokyo   Toronto

and associated companies in
Berlin   Ibadan

Library of Congress Cataloging-in-Publication Data
Allen, Francis A.
The habits of legality : criminal justice and the rule of law /
Francis A. Allen.
p.   cm.—(Studies in crime and public policy)
Includes index.
ISBN 0–19–510088–3
1. Criminal justice, Administration of—United States.
2. Rule of law—United States.   I. Title.   II. Series.
KF9223.A934   1996
345.73′05—dc20   95–15079
[347.3055]

2 4 6 8 9 7 5 3 1

Printed in the United States of America
on acid-free paper

To June, again

Preface

The purpose of this book is to contribute to a holistic view of criminal justice as it exists in late twentieth-century America, by measuring its institutional performance against the requirements of the rule-of-law concept. The discussion does not seek novelty either in the liberal values asserted or in the data considered. The values are not new. They were given expression near the beginning of the modern era in the seventeenth and eighteenth centuries; the legality principle, itself, is one of the most notable products of the liberal revolution of that time. Liberalism, as Learned Hand once suggested, is less a social program or a system of thought than a frame of mind.[1] In modern America, support for liberal values is not robust; the frame of mind is ambiguous and sometimes hostile. As argued in the discussion that follows, attenuation of support in the areas of criminal justice is in significant part a product of certain intellectual currents in the universities, on the one hand, and, on the other, widespread popular attitudes inspired by the perception and reality of epidemic criminality in the United States. It is my hope that identifying and reasserting the importance of the historic values may serve useful purposes in these times.

The content of this volume, revised and somewhat ex-

[1] Letter from Judge Hand to Honorable Charles Fremont Amidon (Feb. 24, 1928), *quoted in part in* G. GUNTHER, LEARNED HAND: THE MAN AND THE JUDGE 443 (1994).

panded, is based on the Cooley Lectures delivered at the University of Michigan Law School on April 5, 6, and 7, 1994. I am grateful to the dean and faculty of the Law School for inviting me to participate in their distinguished lecture series and for providing a warm and memorable homecoming. I am especially grateful to Dean Lee C. Bollinger, who over a long period endured with remarkable patience and good humor the many delays and inconveniences I inflicted on him before the lectures were finally written and delivered. I also express appreciation to the dean and faculty of the University of Arizona Law School and of Mercer University, for earlier providing forums for many of the issues treated in this book.[2]

This volume undertakes discussion of an unusually broad range of topics, most of which have attracted extended scholarly attention over the years. I have, accordingly, found it necessary to rely heavily on the work of others when portraying institutional behavior within the criminal justice system and some of its social consequences. Whenever possible, I have employed documentation to acknowledge my indebtedness, but a number of individuals have made such substantial contributions that additional recognition is required.

The work of Franklin E. Zimring, much of it in collaboration with Gordon Hawkins, has made major contributions of understanding and rationality to the study of criminal justice and has nourished hopes for a genuine policy science in these areas. His observations and data play a prominent role in the pages ahead. Professor Zimring read an early draft of the lectures and offered suggestions that I have attempted, however inexpertly, to incorporate in the text.

Robert S. Summers introduced me to broad areas of jurisprudential literature relevant to my purposes and, with remarkable generosity, supplied helpful criticism and encouragement, particularly in the writing of the first chapter. Sanford H. Kadish read a portion of the manuscript and made valuable suggestions.

---

[2] Allen, *A Crisis of Legality in the Criminal Law?, Reflections on the Rule of Law*, 42 MERCER L. REV. 811 (1991); Allen, *The Erosion of Legality in American Criminal Justice: Some Latter-Day Adventures of the Nulla Poena Principle*, 29 ARIZ. L. REV. 385 (1987).

Terrance Sandalow consented to read my earlier discussions of rule-of-law issues and encouraged me to go forward with the present project. He bears a heavy weight of responsibility. Norval Morris, who has achieved the status of presiding presence over American criminal justice scholarship, has been for me a source of stimulation and insight during 45 years of friendship.

John P. Heinz's article, incorporated in the discussion of chapter 3, was kindly made available to me in manuscript before publication.[3] B. J. George, Jr., furnished copies of his important writings on the Japanese criminal justice system. Professor Jack Beatson of Cambridge University supplied helpful information on the functioning of the English Law Commission and law revision activities elsewhere.

A number of colleagues at the University of Florida College of Law made helpful suggestions: Stuart Cohn, Elizabeth Lear, Winston Nagan, David Richardson, and Christopher Slobogin. As always, the library staffs of the College of Law and of the University of Michigan School of Law provided assistance exceeding expectations. Kristi Jean Kangas, my indefatigable student research assistant, saved me many hours and shamed me by her industry. My profound thanks go to Gwen Reynolds. If there is a more skillful, conscientious, and good-humored secretary in being, I have yet to meet her.

Finally, as in all my enterprises, my wife, June, is the sine qua non.

Ann Arbor, Michigan   F. A. A.
September 1995

---

[3] Heinz & Manikas, *Networks Among Elites in a Local Criminal Justice System*, 26 LAW & SOC. REV. 831 (1992).

Contents

THE HABITS OF LEGALITY

1

The Intellectual Environment
of Legality

The ideal of a political society in which law constrains and guides the exercise of power by rulers dates from the beginnings of systematic thought in the Western world. The rule-of-law phrase is not of ancient lineage. It is said that it was first popularized in the mid-nineteenth century by Albert Venn Dicey, the Vinerian Professor at Oxford and influential commentator on the English Constitution.[1] But the ideal was expressed in the ancient world in various forms of language.[2] Aristotle in his *Politics* writes that

> he who bids the law rule may be deemed to bid God and Reason alone rule, but he who bids man rule adds an element of the beast; for desire is a wild beast, and passion perverts the minds of rulers, even when they are the best of men. The law is reason unaffected by desire.[3]

The last sentence has been translated even more strikingly: "Accordingly law is intelligence without appetite."[4]

Many of the incidents of our political tradition most deeply impressed on our consciousness involved expressions of the rule of law. In Magna Carta the king assures the barons that he will not "proceed with force" against any free man, "except by the lawful judgment of his equals or by the law of the land."[5] In the thirteenth century, Bracton is found asserting that even the king rules *sub Deo et lege,* "under

3

God and the law."[6] More immediately relevant is the career of the concept in seventeenth-century England and in the writings of the eighteenth-century philosophes in Western Europe.[7] It may be forgotten that the notion of a rule of law makes its appearance in modern Western history as a revolutionary doctrine.[8] The American and French Revolutions may in some sense be regarded as its progeny. It is clear, for example, that Beccaria's famous *Essay on Crimes and Punishments,* a forceful eighteenth-century espousal of the rule of law in criminal justice, constitutes a frontal assault on the practices of tyranny in his time.[9]

The rule-of-law concept possesses not only a long historical tradition but also the attributes of encompassing extraordinarily broad areas of public activity and of conveying differing and sometimes conflicting understandings and meanings. It would require an ambition far exceeding the purposes of these remarks to attempt a canvass of all the understandings and applications that have been proposed for the legality ideal. Accordingly, the scope of these comments will be limited to areas that, although broad and of great complexity, occupy only a portion of the terrain ordinarily claimed for the rule of law. At base, the rule of law is concerned with defining the relations between citizens and their government and, to an important extent, the relations of citizens to each other.[10] These remarks, however, are confined almost entirely to problems of containing exercises of power by public officials within applicable legal norms expressed in rules or through other devices that constitute the arsenal of the rule of law.[11] No attention will be given to the role of legality in defining contractual and commercial relations of private parties, although its contributions in stabilizing such relations have historically prompted some of the strongest support for the rule of law. I shall not be concerned primarily with the obligations of citizens, implicit in the rule of law, to demonstrate fidelity and obedience to legitimate law; although, as subsequent remarks may demonstrate, epidemic flouting of the law by members of liberal societies may make difficult, and sometimes impossible, enforcement of the law's obligations on those officials who wield the public force.

The remarks that follow do not deal primarily with the

rights of individuals caught up in the legal process. Such questions are often cognate to the issues now under consideration, and indeed I will argue that respect for the systemic values advanced by the rule of law makes it much more likely that human rights will be respected. The emphasis of my remarks, however, is on the formal aspects of law rather than on substantive rights.[12] Although the two areas are often inextricably intertwined, there are many systemic issues arising from the administration of criminal justice, often neglected and of great importance, that do not immediately and directly impinge on the substantive rights of persons.

Perhaps the most apparent restriction on the scope of the present remarks is that which limits them largely to the areas of criminal justice. The readiest explanation of the limitation, of course, is the restricted competence of the writer. A more substantive case for the focus on criminal justice can perhaps be made. If so, it might well begin with an observation of Montesquieu: "It is . . . on the goodness of criminal laws that the liberty of the subject principally depends," he wrote in *The Spirit of Laws*. "The knowledge already acquired . . . concerning the surest rules to be observed in criminal judgments, is more interesting than any other thing in the world."[13] The statement, calculated to bring joy to teachers of criminal law, merits a moment of serious consideration by others. The legality ideal confronts its sternest tests in the areas of criminal justice for a number of reasons. First, the implications of arbitrary state power are particularly somber here because of the severity of the sanctions administrated by the criminal law and of the status-degrading potency of criminal proceedings. Second, the threat of crime and the outrage it produces often tempt officials to perpetrate and the public to approve carelessness toward, and sometimes disregard of, the legality of their efforts at crime suppression. But more needs to be said. A fundamental end of a legal system in a liberal society is to contribute to conditions consistent with the development of a sturdy sense of autonomy and personhood in its members, individuals capable of directing their own lives and destinies and of making their contributions to civic well-being. These basic objectives are imperiled by rampant criminality and by arbitrary responses of countervailing force by public officers or by laws so uncertain in their meanings and applications as to weaken the sense of security of individual members of society. Moreover, the criminal justice system is the great teacher. What large numbers of the population know or believe about the legal order is derived principally from their observations of and sometimes participation in the criminal justice system. Such impressions therefore are powerful determinants of the levels of fidelity to the law demonstrated by the citizenry. For those tempted to sacrifice the values of legality while pursuing substantive objectives in other areas of public policy, reflections on the effect of such erosions of the rule of law on the administration of criminal justice might well induce sober second thoughts.

Finally, these remarks are not presented as an exercise in jurisprudential analysis. Instead, the focus will be placed on institutional behavior, in an effort to gain more complete understandings of rule-of-law problems disclosed in a functioning legal order, to appraise the vigor of the legality ideal in a broad range of institutional contexts, and to inquire how that vigor may be renewed where it appears at low ebb. Nothing in this effort is intended to challenge the relevance of jurisprudential theory in these areas. Much more of jurisprudential theory and the construction of jurisprudential models relating to the formal aspects of law is required.[14] These remarks reflect a conviction that theoretical constructs in the legal discipline are strengthened and gain enhanced relevance when firmly based on sound understandings of institutional reality; and, indeed, lacking that, theory is often in peril of irrelevancy.[15]

In the course of his ruminations on the rule of law, Dicey assigned first importance to what he called the "predominance of the legal spirit."[16] It was not a new insight. Aristotle long before had offered a similar observation.[17] The rule of law, after all, is a creature of political authority, which is to say that the legality ideal rests on actions and attitudes of public officials whose powers are, in turn, limited and directed by it. It stands in the dual relationship of suspicion toward and dependency on governmental power. The proposition has proved paradoxical to many persons emerging from totalitarian regimes[18] and can be made intelligible only by reference to tradition, spirit, and habit so ingrained in both citizens and public officials as to contain or minimize the perpetual thrust toward aggrandizement of power in the hands of rulers and public officials. Efforts to identify the habits of legality and to measure their vitality, therefore, appear to be among the most important inquiries that can be made about the rule of law in a political society.

For all of the importance of the rule of law in providing a grounding for our traditional legal ideals or, some might say, our traditional piety, an air of unease and even of embarrassment today surrounds discussions of the rule of law in American intellectual circles. The remainder of the chapter will be devoted, first, to identifying and describing certain modern attitudes that in varying degrees have proved antagonistic to the rule-of-law concept and, second, to considering a number of familiar rule-of-law problems and noting how some of the contemporary currents of thought affect their understanding and resolution.

For many modern Americans the legality ideal has largely lost its status as an icon. The concept, on the contrary, is met with a spectrum of attitudes ranging from tentative support to insouciance, skepticism, and even hostility. A measure of skepticism is surely comprehensible. Any citizen awake to the political life of contemporary America will see, in the language of Aristotle, much of "desire" and "appetite" and long for more of "intelligence" and "reason" in the administration of justice, even at the highest levels. The extremes of disillusionment and hostility are another matter, however, and contribute quite different ingredients to the present environment of legality. As we track the rule of law into the morass of actual institutional behavior, we may rarely expect to find expressions of the legality principle in pristine and unqualified forms. Rather, the situation is one in which history, tradition, institutional structure, expediency, and sometimes massive unconcern exert powerful negative pressures on the habits of legality. A certain moral and intellectual toughness is required to attempt invigoration of legality in institutional contexts that doom all efforts of reform to, at best, partial and measured success. The purist stance may create formidable obstacles to progress in such areas, for it fosters the attitude that unless full realization of the legality principle is attainable, all efforts to achieve a more lawful legality are fruitless and naive. Some afflicted with the purist virus retreat into self-created worlds in which contemplation of concepts is unhampered by dismaying realities of institutional behavior.[19]

Yet the present intellectual environment of legality in the United States is not simply the product of those whom H.L.A. Hart described as "disappointed absolutists."[20] The attitudes of the intellectually sophisticated toward the legality principle are of some intricacy, and their importance to the theme of these remarks require that they be given brief attention. We may begin by noting that the rule of law, like other great ideas, has often been trivialized by its ostensible supporters. It has shown itself vulnerable to the bombast and sloganeering of Law Day speeches and commencement addresses. More seriously, it has served as a refuge for scoundrels. Those political figures who speak most insistently about the rule of law in public are often discovered to have been most disposed to dishonor it in private. Such, however is the fate not only of the legality ideal but also of many other of the values important to democratic societies. A value such as privacy, central to the defense of individual autonomy from the reach of state power, has been used as a cloak for privilege and rapacity.[21] Such abuse of fundamental values appears to be one of the persistent attributes of representative democracy, but it hardly serves to render less vital the values so misused.

Perhaps central to the ambivalence displayed toward the legality ideal in these times is what might be called a democratic malaise. Pervasive doubts about the law and its capabilities afflict many of the most responsible members of democratic communities. The doubts put in question the capacities of a turbulent and complex society to achieve its essential objectives when limited by the processes of legal institutions and the letter of the law. The persisting absurdities of legislative lawmaking in the United States and the frequent ineptness of judicial and administrative performance cannot fail to raise questions about the relevance of legal institutions to social requirements. To some persons of suspicious tendencies, the ineptitudes are seen, not simply as fortuitous, but rather as deliberate obstacles to measures that could, it is thought, quickly and effectively respond to human needs—obstacles created by powerful interests hostile to human values. There are large elements of such doubt and suspicion in the thought of many of those who emphasize the achievements of social goals while minimizing or ignoring the claims of legal process.

Yet the claims of law and legal process have survived into the third millennium of Western political experience. Few sober persons in modern democratic societies are prepared to jettison the processes and protections of law, for the twentieth-century world has taught horrific lessons about the consequences of such regression. The result is that many persons of goodwill suffer from a poignant and incapacitating tension[22] produced by the competing claims of "form and substance,"[23] "process and pay-off,"[24] "the morality of means and the morality of ends."[25] The tension adversely affects the habits of legality by tempering protests of official lawlessness seen as furthering useful objectives. It deflects thought and action from reform of our institutional habits in the interests of a more lawful law.

Many of the currents of twentieth-century legal thought in the United States appear to be adverse to traditional understandings of the rule of law. The much-discussed "revolt against formalism" in American social thought, of which the realist movement in the law schools was presumably a prominent feature, may be seen in this light.[26] A listing of the contributions of the realist movement to American legal thought would hardly include the strengthening of the Bractonian view of law as a "bridle of power."[27] Typically, the realists emphasized an inevitable independence of public officials, especially judges, from the constraints of legal rules. Before his later recantation, a younger Karl Llewellyn described legal rules as "pretty playthings."[28] To Jerome Frank, judges professing to be bound by rules and precedent may be seen as displaying neurotic symptoms—psychological afflictions perhaps curable through application of Freudian therapy.[29]

Characteristically, adherents of realist movements, whether in law or other social disciplines, tend to be highly selective of the areas of institutional behavior they choose to be realistic about. Realist jurisprudence counsels skepticism of both the efficacy and desirability of legal rules as determinants of judicial decision making. Even in its less extreme forms, realist jurisprudence gives dominant weight to the judgment and propensities of individual judges in its description of the judicial process. Any complete and authentic description of that process, of course, will take note of the characteristics of individual judges, an insight no doubt widely shared by sophisticated lawyers much before realist jurisprudence emerged as an organized force. Yet a more comprehensive realism might take into account what actual experience and, to a limited degree, scientific inquiry disclose about differences in decision making of persons and groups acting within systems of legal norms and those acting outside such systems.[30] That a rule of law supported by a tradition of legality "makes a difference" in containing the exercise of naked power by public functionaries has again been reaffirmed by scores of observers emerging from behind the Iron Curtain.[31] Moreover, while the proposition that law is what the judges do or, alternatively, predictions of what judges will do may for some purposes possess empirical value, it neglects the significance of antecedent law and hence lacks a conception of law capable of appraising the validity and quality of the behavior of judges or of other public officers.

A prominent feature of the contemporary environment of legality is a widespread language skepticism. In more extreme expressions, skepticism moves to despair about the capacity of language to perform the tasks traditionally assigned to it by the legal system. Concerns about the nature, uses, and limitations of verbal communication must inevitably influence legal theory, even that of the most modest sophistication. Reflective lawyers long before Henry Adams knew that "words are slippery and thought is viscous."[32] Indeed, for 200 years the "cleansing of the verbal state of affairs" in the law has held a central position in the Benthamite tradition.[33] No more forceful attacks on language mystification have been written than those found in Jeremy Bentham's works, and no contemporary polemics show greater awareness than his of the uses of verbal obfuscation as a cloak for tyranny.[34] What distinguishes Bentham's stance from that taken by some modern writers is his faith in language, properly employed, as an instrument for social welfare. For all his indignation at the abuse of language, he did not despair of language as a means of effective legal reform (although the density and eccentricity of his own prose have ever since brought something like despair to readers seeking to penetrate it). His contributions to the modern law of evidence illustrate both his ultimate faith in the capacities of language and his success in employing it for the advancement of rationality and equity in the legal order.[35]

The central point of the modern literature of language indeterminacy appears to be the assertion of a wide, sometimes almost unlimited, freedom in the reader to find his or her own "meanings" in a text. Because of the virtual freedom in the reader to assign meanings to the legal text, we may expect that he or she will choose those meanings that best comport with the reader's own interests and values. Hence "official" readings of legal texts by judges and administrators represent simply the interest of the stronger. Right-minded persons are exhorted to employ their freedom to achieve readings that express their more elevated social values.[36]

It must be clear that theories relating to the communication of understanding are as much theories about the human condition as they are about language. If, indeed, human capacities to communicate are so limited that understandings of readers and auditors cannot ordinarily be confined within a relatively narrow spectrum of alternatives, then there emerges an even more atomistic picture of the human species than we may have suspected heretofore. It presents a picture of discrete individuals separated by walls of incomprehension. We may be compelled to reject John Donne's assurance that "no man is an island." Not only does the view imply separation from other human beings now living, but it, a fortiori, bars us from understanding the past.[37] One wonders how such a view can escape dissonance with a social philosophy that places high value on community and on human interaction.

The literature of language indeterminacy often appears to give inadequate recognition to the widely differing purposes among the various kinds of verbal texts. The notions of "meaning" and "communication" must surely be different to a reader approaching a Vladimir Nabokov novel from one confronting the Internal Revenue Code.[38] The reader approaching a legal text does so, not to construct a personal world of his own making, but ordinarily to be able to make authentic statements about what the law is as it relates to a situation or a course of action.[39] In accepting the latter purpose, the reader is subjected to a range of institutional constraints of a kind absent in other contexts. Moreover, differences of purposes among verbal texts are not confined to broad categories like those of creative literature and of law. Different kinds of legal texts define significantly differing roles for their readers.[40] Interpreting the broad mandates of the Constitution may require a different quality of readership from that demanded in seeking the meaning of a commercial lease or contract.

The modern expressions of pessimism concerning the capacities of ordinary language to perform the functions of guidance and restraint of official power seem overdrawn and incompletely supported. We need not ignore the acute fallibilities of verbal communication to recognize that there are differences between a well-drafted and a poorly drafted statute or commercial document. Nor does there seem to be reason to ignore the fact that in the routine work of the world the law often proceeds at tolerable levels of satisfaction, despite the limitations of language. There seems no reason to doubt that increasing demands will be placed on the language of the law in the future. We may expect that in the increasingly aggressive pluralism, indeed polarization, of American society, smaller reliance on commonly held, unspoken norms of personal and public behavior will be possible and that increased dependence on articulated standards, many in the form of authoritative legal rules, will be required.

Linguistic theory and the fruits of linguistic research are important and legitimate resources for modern legal scholarship. Given the centrality of linguistic issues to the legal order, any contributions to their better understanding and more satisfactory resolution should not be neglected. What is needed, however, are changes in the focus and objectives of much legal scholarship in these areas. Sweeping assertions of the incapacities of language, with their implied pessimism about the possibilities of limited government and the attainability of law, have been present in overabundance. All too little attention has been given to the resources of ordinary language and how they may be employed for more effective communication in the myriad particular situations in which the legal order is required to act. Such inquiry is overdue and its potential is promising.[41]

It is clear that in much academic writing at present there exist nihilistic strains incompatible with the assumptions on which law and the rule of law rest. The circumstance must be noted in any effort to portray the environment of legality in American society. Yet trends in current academic writing constitute only part of the atmosphere and, as subsequent remarks may suggest, not necessarily the most important part. Moreover, the academic posture toward the rule of law is more frequently one of skepticism than hostility. It seems likely that the great majority in the academic community, including those individuals most aware of continuing failures to achieve full expression of the legality ideal, strongly prefer to live in a society that includes the rule of law among its aspirations, however unfulfilled, than in one in which the ideal is frontally assaulted and deliberate measures are taken to subvert it.

It cannot be ignored, however, that individuals and groups in some American academic communities, emphatically reject the legality ideal and denounce the rule of law as little more than a cloak to camouflage the oppressions of a rapacious capitalist society.[42] The position seems to be based in large measure on the insight that law may be conscripted by oppressive regimes, and when this occurs the rule of law may be employed for oppressive ends. It would be wrong to deny that in American society, law has sometimes been employed for ends degrading to human dignity and autonomy. The support given by state and federal courts in the first half of this century to "private" systems of racial residential segregation, for example, constitutes a dark page in American legal history.[43] The motivations of individuals possessed of a vision of a more benign society and one more inclusive of persons to share its benefits are entitled to respect. But in seeking to realize the vision by eroding the systems of thought and the institutional foundations on which the rule of law rests, the critics are proposing an enormous wager. The gamble is that the vision can be achieved through the weakening of such devices as we possess to contain the rule of unfettered political power. The reasonableness of such expectations seems wholly unsupported by historical experience, and most persons therefore are likely to conclude that the wager cannot responsibly be made.

II

The environment of legality at the present moment in the United States is the product of more than current trends in legal literature. It is defined in significant part by the circumstances that have confronted the administration of criminal justice for more than a generation and by popular response and public measures taken in consequence. Nevertheless, the current intellectual postures cannot be dismissed as inconsequential. The discussion now moves to a number of practical issues encountered in applying the legality principle to criminal justice administration and to a consideration of how the vitality of the ideal in some such cases may be affected by certain modern attitudes.

The notion of the rule of law is one that seeks to impose limits on and provide guidance for the exercise of official power. We can conceive of exertions of governmental authority that are legal in the sense of being authorized by law but that offend the rule-of-law concept. If a political society could be supposed in which the constitution authorizes the ruler to govern with complete caprice, the results of the ruler's arbitrary fiats, in the view of some, might not constitute law at all; they certainly would not constitute the rule of law.[44] The central concept of limitation contributed by the rule of law to the criminal process is expressed in the familiar principle, appropriately ensconced in Latin, *Nulla poena sine lege,* "No punishment without [preexisting] law."[45] The proposition that persons ought not be subjected to the stigmatic sanctions of the criminal law who at the time of acting were denied knowledge that their behavior risked punishment may appear so obvious as to be hardly interesting. The principle is deceptively simple. For most persons it immediately suggests the constitutional prohibitions of ex post facto laws. The classic ex post facto case, of course, does grossly offend the *nulla poena* principle; but such cases in Western industrial societies constitute only a minuscule portion of the situations in which the principle requires attention.[46] Thus, as will subsequently be noted more fully, the practice of plea bargaining impinges on the principle because it often results in the application, not of preexisting law, but rather of law created at the point of application. Freewheeling interpretations of criminal statutes in appellate courts give rise to issues beyond the separation of governmental powers and include problems of retrospective lawmaking. The *nulla poena* principle is of prime concern, for it implicates central values of liberal societies. A significant part of the dignity of individuals as they confront the power of the state is their ability to assert effectively that guilt is personal, that they are immune from criminal accountability for consequences they did not cause and for acts they could not have known were or would be condemned by political authority. These immunities represent more than devices to advance economic enterprise or even to create a comfortable feeling of security. As Professor Summers has written,

> If . . . persons are punished under laws they could not have known about when acting, this not merely undermines the preconditions of informed choice and planning, it also disregards the limits of human responsibility and is therefore both unfair and an affront to human dignity. Thus, the values that cluster about predictability are not merely instrumental.[47]

Although the point seems not often made, the *nulla poena* principle has important implications not only for the procedures of justice but also for the substantive criminal law. It speaks to the questions, What is a crime? and Who is the criminal? The *nulla poena* concept assumes that persons become criminals because of their acts, not simply because of who or what they are. One purpose of fair notice to the community, explicit in the principle, is to ensure opportunities for its members to avoid criminal sanctions by adapting their conduct to the law's requirements. Such opportunities were denied members of totalitarian societies by decrees criminalizing the racial or ethnic status of the accused or their political or ideological antecedents. There emerged both in the former Soviet Union and in Nazi Germany a doctrine of "criminal types," reminiscent of positivist criminology in the late-nineteenth century.[48] As the Soviet commentator Eugenii Pashukanis expressed it, the task of criminal adjudication is less that of establishing the elements of a crime in a particular case than of detecting "symptoms" of a socially dangerous condition in the accused and of devising appropriate measures of social defense in response. Comparable attitudes are evident in the writings of Nazi jurists.[49] Nor is the problem confined to political dictatorships. The tendency to criminalize status rather than conduct is evident in centuries of vagrancy prosecutions in the Anglo-American legal system.[50] It is the disposition of penal rehabilitationism to focus on what the offender is thought to be rather than on what he has done that prompted much of the most acute criticism of the rehabilitative ideal when it dominated thought in American corrections for the larger part of the present century.[51]

Persons who have scanned the 1980s' "security laws" of the Republic of South Africa[52] or have reviewed even hastily the penal decrees and accompanying juristic writings in the former Soviet Union and in Nazi Germany[53] cannot fail to be impressed by the deliberation with which these productions were framed to destroy the essential elements of political liberty. It may fairly be assumed that those aspects of legal and political institutions selected as primary targets of assault by authoritarian regimes to achieve their dictatorial aims are likely to be among the most important to the life of societies valuing individual autonomy. Measured by this test, the rule of law and, in particular, the *nulla poena* principle are identified as of prime importance. The Nazi conception of law, stripped of its mystical trappings, was purely instrumental. Law was only one of a large number of devices to achieve the purposes of the state as discerned by the Nazi leader, certainly not one to curtail or define his uses of authority or those of his subordinate officers. In the famous Act of June 28, 1935, the *nulla poena* principle was emphatically rejected, the culmination of a development that had its origins, it is said, in the Weimar Republic.[54] An even more open-ended formulation was made part of the Russian Penal Code of 1926.[55]

The point need not be labored that the requirement of a preexisting criminal law, articulated by the *nulla poena* principle, cannot be satisfied by secret law or law written in a language foreign to the population to which it applies.[56] The principle posits communication of law to those who may be affected by it. Communication in turn entails laws widely published, freely accessible to the populace, and expressed in terms intelligible to it. These propositions seem obvious enough, yet the role of courts in after-the-act interpretation of criminal statutes remains one of the most acute rule-of-law issues in contemporary America. In certain areas of the criminal process, notably corrections, the principle of communication of rules and penal regulations to inmate populations is often slighted, sometimes deliberately so;[57] and parole boards often fail to give reasons for their actions from which principles of their decision making might be inferred.[58] Moreover, the accessibility of law in the conditions of modern social life must mean more than publication of statutes and judicial opinions and their availability in law libraries. Frequently reasonable and good-faith efforts to discover what the law is fail, and persons find themselves in violation of penal regulations the existence of which they were unaware or the application to themselves they had no reason to suspect. Mistakes of law of this kind, the likelihood of which increases in a penal system that has sharply extended its regulations into areas not theretofore regarded as within the domain of the criminal law, represent failures to achieve the necessary communication between lawmakers and citizens, posited by the *nulla poena* principle. The unwillingness of many courts in the United States to withhold penal sanctions in such cases suggests an attitude that the rule of law may be a luxury too expensive to afford.[59] Strict criminal liability involving nonnegligent mistakes of fact give rise to related concerns.

The rule of law encompasses more than the articulation and accessibility of laws; it is necessarily concerned with the interpretation and application of law. Accordingly, independence of the judiciary from executive domination has been universally associated with the legality principle in the modern era.[60] Not surprisingly, the suppression of that independence became a prime objective of the Nazi regime. Criminal tribunals and the judges who presided over them were seen simply as agencies to achieve the political and military objectives of the state, a position encapsulated in an observation by a high official of the Ministry of Justice: "The apolitical, neutral judge of the liberal multiparty state, who stands on the sidelines, must become a National Socialist with sure instincts and a feeling for the great political aims of the movement. Politics, philosophy, and justice are one and the same."[61] The implications of an independent judiciary, however, extend beyond avoidance of gross interference by the executive in the performance of judicial functions. Judges are granted independence, in part, freely to apply the rule of law. Judges who voluntarily surrender their freedom and adhere to the supposed interests of executive power at the expense of the rule of law subvert the necessary independence of the judiciary. Unfortunately, some judges in an era of great and understandable concern about crime and its suppression have been induced to sacrifice their freedom to be guided by the rule of law.[62]

In his well-known list of factors that prevent the achievement of law, the late Lon Fuller included "the failure of congruence between rules as announced and their actual administration."[63] Such failures of correspondence between rules and their applications may be the products of many and widely differing deficiencies, but of primary importance is the absence of a process and procedure capable of fair and reasonably reliable adjudication of criminal charges. It is at the point of application of the criminal law that many of the most flagrant abuses were perceived by eighteenth-century reformers like Voltaire and Beccaria, and the elimination of such abuse became a principal motivation for elevating the rule of law to a central position in what might be called the liberal revolution of that era.[64] Fair trial and the entire panoply of procedural due process are important not only to the achievement of justice in particular cases but also to the realization of legality throughout the system. The American constitutional scheme of basic rights assumes the functioning of a vigorous adversary system of criminal justice. Important reliance is placed on the effective operation of the system for the guidance and containment of official force. It follows that factors that cripple the functioning of the adversary system constitute threats to the legality ideal. One such factor is the characteristic poverty of the criminally accused and the frequent inability or unwillingness of the community to supply the indigent with adequate legal services, even when the state is seeking the life of the accused.[65] Adequate and legitimate resistance to official accusations of crime is essential to protect the rights and interests of individuals caught up in the toils of criminal prosecutions, but it is equally important in satisfying basic systemic concerns.[66]

As would be expected, the Nazi instinct for the jugular of liberal societies brought forth measures limiting, if not wholly eliminating, the independence of lawyers defending criminal cases. The Minister of Justice, Otto Thierick, was instructed by Hitler that the defense lawyer must be "a person representing the state."[67] The view was applauded by at least some members of the bar, one of whom asserted: "Just as the new trial no longer represents a conflict between the interests of an individual and the state, now the legal participants should regard their tasks no longer opposed to one another, but rather as a joint effort infused with a spirit of mutual trust."[68] Just how far the "mutual trust" could go is indicated by the speeches delivered by defense counsel in opposition to their clients in the Reichstag fire prosecution and by the defense attorney who urged the death penalty for General Erich Hoeppner in the 1944 military trial following the attempted assassination of Hitler.[69]

The rule of law is only one of the devices to direct and contain the powers of public officials, available to a political society valuing individual autonomy. The mores and morals of the community, widely held and often unarticulated, are, of course, fundamental. The ballot box in a democratic society may represent the ultimate remedy for widespread official disregard of legal norms. The ethics of professionalism may, on occasion, prevent or moderate excesses of public officers. In certain institutional settings, like those in which public prosecutors in Japan operate, professional tradition and morale may be more important than formal rules, guidelines, or administrative oversight in determining the standards of official behavior.[70] Yet none of these alone or in combination is sufficient to the task. The public sense of propriety is regularly flouted by public officials, sometimes with apparent impunity. Political campaigns are rarely concerned with the host of low-visibility erosions of legality that cumulatively sap the vitality of public norms, and changes of personnel in public office may not reduce unauthorized uses of public authority.[71] The ethics of professionalism, often of great importance in minimizing excess, may in some situations exacerbate a tendency to disregard restraints on public power. That this excessive use of public power may occur is demonstrated not only by the Nazi experience[72] but also by the history of penal rehabilitationism in the United States when serious invasions of human dignity and rights were regularly defended as instances of professional treatment.[73]

The central devices of the rule of law are rules that prohibit certain options of official behavior or that mandate certain kinds of official action. The rules may be more or less "open-textured," as H.L.A. Hart has put it, permitting the public officer limited options.[74] Indeed, some areas of legal regulation are of a nature that makes creation of formal rules unfeasible, in which case resort may be had to broad guidelines for official action or less formal modes of control.[75] Enforcement of rules of whatever description may take a wide variety of forms. Certain kinds of official action in violation of legal norms may give rise to criminal prosecution of the offender, as provided by civil rights legislation.[76] Other sorts of norm violation by public officers may result in preventing the use of otherwise competent evidence in criminal trials. Disregard of rules may deprive some official acts of legal efficacy. Other kinds of rule violations may subject the officer to disciplinary sanctions by an agency vested with powers of administrative oversight.

Lon Fuller wrote that the most basic cause of the failure of a political society to achieve law is the failure to achieve rules at all.[77] Clearly, whatever contributions the rule of law may be expected to make to the containment and direction of official power rests in large part on rules that remove certain options of conduct from public officials. Yet formal rules have served as the focal point of much of the current skepticism and hostility expressed in American academic writing. In part the attitudes are products of widespread assumptions about the indeterminacy and incapacities of language, mentioned above. Language skepticism gives rise to rule skepticism. The persuasiveness of the linguistic analysis, however, is hardly so overpowering as to provide a full explanation of current attitudes. Indeed, a very different complaint about formal rules is made that objects, not to the indeterminacy of rules, but rather to their efficacy. Rules are feared precisely because they sometimes deny options—to public officials, especially to judges—that may be thought to produce wiser and more just outcomes.

Over a half century ago, the late Max Radin expressed his aspiration for "a more just justice" and "a more lawful law."[78] Current academic attitudes, sometimes shared by a wider public, are strongly inclined to see the two objectives as antagonistic rather than as harmonious and complementary. Rules must always contend with the power of the concrete case, and even when rules are stated with the greatest possible clarity, forces may be generated to accommodate the particular equities presented. The resistance to government by rules in the interests of what is seen as individualized justice emerges at every level of the criminal process—in policing, in exercising prosecutorial powers, in adjudicating and sentencing. Often the pressures result from a search for a more perfect proportionality between the culpability of the offender and the societal response to his or her dereliction than is thought possible within the confines of applicable rules. The tendency is strengthened by the frequent ineptness displayed in the form and substance of rules as they emerge from American legislatures, courts, and sentencing commissions. The consequences include resistance to introduction of formal rules in areas of administration where they do not now exist and in strategies of avoidance when rules are in place.

The tension between rules and aspirations for individualized justice is a pervasive, and perhaps inevitable, attribute of liberal societies and one by no means wholly to be regretted. The tension can be identified even in the substantive criminal law, the domain in which the case for general rules of certain application is the strongest. Even here the unique facts of the particular situation may condition the generality of rules. The concept of criminal negligence, for example, has never been fully defined. The negligence formula establishes wide parameters and invokes the fact-finder's judgment formed in response to the unique circumstances presented. The defense of the "lesser evil," articulated in statutory form in the Model Penal Code, validates disobedience of penal commands on ad hoc determinations by courts that the accused's failures to comply produced lesser evils than would have been created had the law been obeyed.[79] The continuing critique of general rules by persons advancing the claims of individualized justice has often resulted in a criminal law more humane and more ingenious in accommodating the claims of individualized equity. What is troubling about current academic attitudes is a tendency toward the uninhibited advocacy of the claims of individualized justice whenever those objectives appear to be in any way limited by rules of general application. The ready, almost unthinking, willingness to sacrifice the rule of law in such instances may exact serious costs. There has been little disposition to measure such costs or even to recognize that they exist. Among the costs is the weakening of what may be called the normative values of formal legality—certainty, predictability, equality of treatment, and avoidance of arbitrary exercises of official authority. It is well to be aware that not all of those who chafe under a regime of formal rules are persons who seek a system of penal justice scrupulous of the equities of the individual accused. Freeing public officers of the constraints of formal legality may be motivated by quite different agendas. Persons who complain that constitutional restraints are "handcuffing the police" do not urge unlocking the fetters in order that a nicer sense of justice for the individual offender may be displayed. On the contrary, what is most often sought is a harsher, more undiscriminating and unregulated use of the public force. Those seeking a more sensitive and humane criminal justice in these times may be well advised to value the habits of legality.

At least as important to the system of criminal justice as questions regarding the problematic nature of formal rules or of their efficacy are those that surround the exercise of discretion by public officials. That decisions undetermined and largely uninfluenced by rules of any description abound in the criminal process is a fact easily corroborated by even superficial observation of institutional behavior. Many such decisions affect the interests of individuals in the most direct and devastating fashion and are made at all levels of the criminal process from police patrol on city streets through completion of the correctional process in the prisons or the administration of parole. Discretionary power in public officials incurred the hostility of earlier exponents of the rule of law. The widely quoted strictures of Lord Camden are illustrative. In 1705 he observed, in part: "The Discretion of a Judge is the Law of Tyrants."[80] Leon Duguit more recently asserted in his treatise on constitutional law, "No organ of the state may render an individual decision which would not conform to a general rule previously stated."[81] The hostility of Dicey to discretionary power is well known.[82]

In the modern era those who see merit in strengthening the habits of legality are confronted by a more complex problem. It is no longer possible simply to deplore discretionary decision making. The problem today is to come to terms with it and to do so in a fashion that preserves as much as possible of the essential ingredients of the legality ideal. In the period immediately following the Vietnam War, there were those who, for a time, believed that the inequities of the criminal process could be remedied simply by crafting a system that denied discretionary powers to its principal actors.[83] The egalitarian impulse of the 1970s failed in its objective, and it may unwittingly have made aspirations of individualized justice more difficult to attain. Recognizing the inevitability of discretionary authority in Western societies is not grounded on unawareness that disturbing abuses of discretionary power characterize modern history nor on ignorance of the difficulties in modern conditions of identifying officials responsible for such abuse and holding them accountable. The essential claim for discretionary power rests on the fact that basic social objectives cannot be gained without it. It is often indispensable to the achieving of what needs to be done and what members of the society desire to have done.[84] In the system of criminal justice, as elsewhere, the task, then, becomes one of determining where and by whom discretion is being exercised, what discretionary powers are, in fact, essential to basic social purposes, and how the exercise of those powers may be guided and contained so as to give meaning to essential social values rather than to weaken or to destroy them.

The task is formidable. The very scale of the problem is daunting. Mortimer Kadish and Sanford Kadish have identified certain areas of institutional operation in which persons or agencies have been made subject to legal rules but in which those performing the legal functions are granted a freedom to disregard the legal norms. This is done by not penalizing the functionaries or impairing the legal efficacy of their acts; hence, there is created a "discretion to disobey."[85] The freedom of juries to disregard instructions of judges provides one example, but a number of others are identified. In many such instances the functionaries are confronted by what appear to be conflicts in the purposes of the legal order, and in a few the freedom is the product of something approaching a conscious calculation that community interests are advanced by tolerating the freedom rather than by suppressing it. The larger problem is of a different order. It is less that of disregard of official norms than of sometimes total absence of governing norms. An apparent normlessness—or perhaps better, an anarchy of competing and unarticulated values—characterizes American criminal justice in many of its most important aspects and often strongly affects the lives and welfare of persons. It is here that the "failure to achieve rules at all" is most clearly displayed.

A complete and satisfying explanation of the widespread normlessness prevailing in broad sectors of American criminal justice would include a range of social and political factors extending much beyond the penal system itself. A number of the factors will be noted in the discussions that follow. At present only two of the salient elements will be mentioned. First, the American experience has resulted in a penal system highly localized and fragmented, one largely lacking in traditions of centralized oversight comparable to those prevailing in most other industrialized nations. As will be argued in chapter 3, institutions of justice, as they have evolved in the United States, often fail to provide for adequate scrutiny of public officials' behavior or to impose appropriate accountability for official misconduct. It is also essential to note that because of their nature, variety, and complexity, many criminal justice functions do not lend themselves to governance by codes of formal rules. In many such areas more general rule-of-law constraints—guidelines, strategies of administrative oversight—are largely untried, and their efficacy therefore is in doubt. In the United States, systematic thought directed to identifying the areas in which stringent legality controls are indispensable, more relaxed scrutiny may be permissible, or restraints cannot successfully be attempted is only beginning to find a place in the mainstream of criminal law scholarship and, accordingly, exists in early stages of development.[86]

Efforts to reform American criminal justice in the interest of a fuller expression of the legality ideal constitute an enterprise attended by difficulties and perils. Attempts to contain discretionary decision making in a given area may fail because inadequate attention has been given to the interrelatedness of the function in question with the operations of the justice system as a whole. Intervention in the internal operations of systems may breed defensive reactions that frustrate well-intended objectives of reform. The specter of the unintended and unanticipated consequence hovers over the reform enterprise. Yet the case for intelligent reform is insistent. Its object should be a system of justice in which unregulated exertions of public authority are tolerated only after rational calculation demonstrates that societal interests are better served by toleration than by attempts at suppression.

That the American system of criminal justice in practice departs radically from such a description is clear to anyone conversant with the operation of its institutions. Where and how unsupervised discretion is being exercised may often be unknown even to many of those participating in the institution's functions. Freedom from scrutiny and consequent unaccountability of public officers are typically products, not of rational calculation, but rather of accidents of institutional development. Such practices, once established feed on themselves. They respond to a perverse public desire that as many of the grubby realities of criminal justice administration as possible be kept out of sight and hence out of mind. A tendency to resort to unguided discretion as a means to avoid confronting basic issues of public policy has often impeded the rational reform of institutional practices.[87] Frequently, in efforts to recodify the substantive criminal law, for example, proposals to introduce important distinctions into crime definitions are met with impatient retorts that such complications are unnecessary, because sentencing judges can be relied on to take them into account and give them appropriate weight. Yet as modern statutory law reform of the last generation demonstrates, much fuller articulation of relevant principles and distinctions in the statutory criminal law is entirely feasible, and the result is a body of criminal legislation more fully defined and closer to the spirit of the *nulla poena* principle than were earlier tacit delegations of authority to the discretionary sentencing powers of judges.[88] Part of the case for an expanded role for the legality ideal is that it contributes a greater rationality to both law and process. In the administration of criminal justice, at least, we may discover that a quest for a more just justice must, indeed, be joined by a search for a more lawful law.

These remarks have advanced the proposition that the functional meaning of the rule of law in an operating society is in large part a product of the habits of legality displayed in the behavior of political institutions and in the levels of fidelity to the law and the concept of legality expressed in the conduct of its members. Some, but by no means all, important tendencies in modern academic writing in the United States contribute to an intellectual environment hardly invigorating to the habits of legality. Much theoretical writing assumes postures indifferent to the normative values of the rule of law and careless of the consequences of their neglect.

Description of the environment of legality demands more, however, than scrutiny of academic trends of thought. American law enforcement since the 1960s has been called on to grapple with an array of the most extraordinary circumstances and conditions and, in doing so, has raised serious questions about the vitality of the legality ideal in contemporary criminal justice and its future role. In addition, older and more persistent issues of governmental structure and historical predispositions must be confronted. It is to these matters that attention will be directed in the next two chapters.

2

The Institutional Environment
of Legality

Habits of legality manifested in the administration of criminal justice are products of a wide variety of influences. One of the most important of these is the level of unease produced in the community by the perceived threats to life, limb, and property arising from criminal activity. The fear of crime encompasses the most basic and primitive human concerns and, if widespread and acute, may create a crisis of confidence in the capacities of legal institutions to perform their essential functions. In such periods concerns about abuses of governmental authority by police, prosecutors, and judicial officers, as they wield the most stringent sanctions of government, tend to be engulfed in the deeper fears of criminal victimization. At such times the traditions of legality are not wholly or suddenly abandoned, but the social and political environment is one increasingly unfavorable to the habits of legality.

Periods of intense concern about the prevalence and seriousness of crime have emerged at frequent intervals throughout our history. Indeed, one of the most acute and portentous manifestations of such unease arose in the years immediately following the American Revolution.[1] In the past, such periods were short lived; public attention was soon diverted by other apparently more pressing problems and crises. Typically, also, the problems perceived tended to

be viewed as new and unprecedented, earlier episodes of
similar concerns having been largely forgotten.[2] There is
reason to believe that the present era of intense public disquiet differs from earlier episodes in several important respects. First is the persistence and duration of current public
agitations. Acute concerns about the incidence and seriousness of crime have constituted an important part of American social and political life for over a generation. Other
issues, of course, have from time to time successfully com-
peted for public attention in the dangerous years since the
mid-1960s, but a steady and often intense current of unease
about the problems of crime has persisted throughout the
entire period. Moreover, the present era is unique in the
number and scope of legislative and administrative measures taken to combat crime in its various forms, the efforts
coming to a kind of climax in the years since 1980.

For the purposes at hand, the present era in the history of
American criminal justice may be seen to date from the administration of President Lyndon Johnson. Indeed, the important reports and recommendations of the President's
Commission on Law Enforcement and the Administration of
Justice, issued in the late 1960s and intended to provide
blueprints for criminal justice policy in the years ahead, instead mark the end of a penal policy in the criminal area
based on the principles of liberal politics and seeking to
achieve not only crime repression but also, in some measure, social reconciliation.[3] The efforts of the Commission to
shape and direct penal policy were not wholly without benefit,[4] but its spirit and basic recommendations were quickly
ignored and largely forgotten. From that date forward, the
objectives of criminal justice in the United States became
almost exclusively those of repression and incapacitation, the mood of the endeavor having been captured early
in the era by President Richard Nixon's metaphor of a war
between what he called the "peace forces" and the "criminal
forces."[5]

Public attitudes toward and official reactions to the phenomena of crime during the last generation are not simply
capricious and incomprehensible. On the contrary, they represent responses to an inescapable reality, a reality typically
ignored or underestimated by the liberal wing of American

politics for much of the period in question.[6] For however misconceived by the public, manipulated by politicians, or distorted and exploited by the media, the fact of rampant criminality and the specter of violent crime constitute a reality all too concrete and alarming in American society. Their effect on the habits of legality practiced by public officials is correspondingly tangible.

To explore this effect we may well begin by noting the scale of the problems with which the institutions of criminal justice are being called on to contend. American law enforcement and corrections are staggering under an enormous weight of numbers—numbers of crimes, of criminals and victims, of prosecutions and appeals, of prisoners and prisons.[7] The dangers and dilemmas of the present era encompass much more than the problems of scale. But the weight of numbers, alone, has proved more than sufficient to nurture reactions erosive of the legality principle.

Persons living in American society at any time since the late 1960s will have acquired some sense, however inexact, of the burdens being borne by the system of criminal justice. Only a sketch of their dimensions can be presented here. In 1992 the estimated number of murders and nonnegligent homicides committed in the United States was 23,760—a rate of 9.3 per 100,000 population.[8] The number of robberies was estimated at almost 700,000. There were believed to have been over a million aggravated assaults and approximately 3 million burglaries.[9] More than 14 million arrests were estimated to have been made in the United States in 1992, more than 700,000 of these for violent crimes and more than 2 million for crimes against property.[10] Victimization studies indicate that in 1992, one in four American households sustained a crime of violence or theft.[11] By the end of 1992 the population of state and federal prisons had risen to 883,593—an increase of 7.9% over what had been the record high in the previous year.[12] Since 1968, near the beginning of the era now under consideration, the number of persons incarcerated in prisons and penitentiaries had expanded some four-and-a-half times, and the rate of imprisonment per unit of population by some 260%.[13] In addition, American jails hold about 450,000 inmates, so that persons confined in penal custodial institutions at the end of

1992 numbered well over a million.[14] When these numbers are added to those of offenders subjected to some form of supervised release like probation or parole, the total reaches beyond 4 million persons, a figure larger than the population of any of 29 American states.[15] One out of four black males between the ages of 18 and 30 in the United States is being subjected to some variety of penal restraint.[16]

Statistics of the sort just stated are part of the familiar journalistic grist and may be more likely to produce numbness than enlightenment. Comprehension of their magnitude may be assisted when we compare a few of the numbers reported in the United States with those generated in other industrialized nations. During the last generation, many other countries, like the United States, experienced epidemics of criminal violence and rising crime rates; and some reacted to the phenomena in ways recognizably similar to our own.[17] The factor that sharply distinguishes American from foreign experience, however, is the magnitude of the problems implicit in the American statistics. In the late 1980s the rate of imprisonment in England and Wales—90.3 prisoners per 100,000 population—exceeded that of almost all European countries, a fact that, when known, produced considerable local disquiet and public agitation.[18] At the same time, however, the rate of imprisonment in the United States as a whole was more than four times that in England and Wales.[19] At the beginning of the 1990s the prison systems of California and New York each held more inmates in confinement than did any nation of Western Europe.[20] In 1989 about twice as many murders were committed in New York City alone as were reported for all of England and Wales.[21] The murder rate in Japan was recently reported to be 1.1 per 100,000 inhabitants; that in the United States is at least nine times greater.[22]

The reality that emerges from such numbers and comparisons greatly affects virtually all aspects of American social and political life. For the purposes at hand, primary attention will be given to the effects produced by the weight of numbers on the nature and functioning of the justice system. It appears clear, at the outset, that the dramatic increase of criminal cases on the dockets of state and federal courts has adversely affected the capacity of courts to administer both criminal and civil justice effectively. The inundation of drug prosecutions in the federal courts and its impact on their civil dockets are illustrative. The number of accused persons sentenced to prison in federal district courts grew from about 17,500 in 1982 to 33,600 in 1992.[23] The infusion of unprecedented numbers of criminal prosecutions into the federal judicial system has severely restricted its ability to accommodate a growing docket of civil cases.[24] Some of the consequences are summarized in the *Report of the Federal Courts Study Committee* in 1990:

> Drug filings not only increase the federal court workload; they distort it. The Speedy Trial Act[25] in effect requires that the federal courts give criminal cases priority over civil cases. As a result, some districts with heavy drug caseloads are virtually unable to try civil cases and others will soon be at that point. And when courts cannot set realistic trial dates, parties lose much of their incentive to settle and civil cases drag on in limbo.[26]

The surge of drug prosecutions in the federal courts during the decade and a half just past has modified, some may say distorted, the functioning of other public institutions in significant and unanticipated ways. The impact of drug law enforcement on the prosecution policy of the Internal Revenue Service (IRS) may be one of these. The number of drug and related cases recommended for prosecution under the federal tax laws by the IRS's criminal enforcement division grew 337% in the decade of the 1980s, while recommendations for criminal proceedings against otherwise legitimate business people fell by 30%.[27] It is said that in these years the amount of investigative time devoted by the enforcement division on general tax cases declined from 75% to 50%.[28] These changes, for many, threaten a weakening of the capacity of the IRS to protect the federal revenues. Such was the view expressed in a study undertaken by a committee of the American Bar Association's Tax Section in 1991. The report asserts:

> Our criminal enforcement system is rapidly losing its ability to deter otherwise law abiding taxpayers from cheating on their obligations. Tax prosecutions of drug dealers . . . and other notorious offenders do little, if anything, to foster voluntary

compliance with the tax laws among the large majority who earn their incomes legitimately, which is and should remain the goal of criminal tax enforcement. Absent some quick and decisive redirection of efforts, the long term stability of our voluntary compliance system could be seriously jeopardized.[29]

The performance of the judicial function in criminal cases has been significantly affected by the weight of numbers, sometimes in ways that can be discerned if not precisely measured. The functioning of appellate courts provides apt illustrations. As would be expected, there has been a striking increase in the number of criminal appeals during the last generation. In the United States courts of appeal, for example, criminal filings are said to have expanded by a factor of more than 10 in the years 1960–1989.[30] One of the consequences of the inundation appears to be an increasingly dubious resort to the doctrine of "harmless error."[31]

A study conducted in the 1980s of the harmless-error concept as utilized in a state appellate court supports the conclusion that despite the more-rigorous restrictions on public authority that ostensibly surround the determination of criminal guilt, the procedural standards actually enforced by many appellate courts are higher in civil than in criminal cases.[32] Very likely, a reluctance to return criminal cases for retrial in a period of crowded criminal dockets is one influence at work here, a reluctance making understandable Justice Thurgood Marshall's protest that "[i]f appellate review is to be meaningful, it must fulfill its basic historic function of correcting error in trial court proceedings."[33]

Among the many deleterious consequences of the numbers oppressing American criminal justice, none is more important than those affecting the nature and functioning of the adversary process.[34] In no other industrial nation has so great a reliance been placed on the contest between prosecution and defense as in the United States, not only to protect the interests of particular individuals accused of crime but also to erect a system of challenge and restraint calculated to contain the public force in a broad range of governmental operations. In such a system the role of lawyers for the defense is crucial, for in large measure defense counsel must be relied on to supply the challenges that the system presupposes.[35] This fact, sometimes overlooked in the United

States, was thoroughly understood by the Nazi regime and accounts for its assiduous efforts to neutralize the role of defense attorneys in criminal proceedings.[36]

There can be little doubt that the element of challenge has been considerably muted in American criminal justice in the recent past and that the tendency in some measure reflects the weight of numbers on the system. The impact, of course, is manifested in many different ways. One of the most obvious of these has been already referred to: the failure of American systems of criminal justice in an era of rapidly proliferating criminal prosecutions to supply adequate legal representation of accused persons unable to provide for themselves. Despite constitutional mandates identifying effective legal representation as an indispensable ingredient of fair trial, the legal assistance supplied in many American courts, 60 years after the decision of the Supreme Court in *Powell v. Alabama,* sometimes consists of hardly more than pious ritual.[37] The reluctance of appellate courts to upset criminal convictions obtained in proceedings flawed by seriously deficient legal representation of the criminally accused, a conservatism that is itself in part a product of pressures of numbers on appellate dockets, seriously exacerbates the situation.[38] In consequence of these and other factors, challenges generated by the defense to the most stringent exertions of the public force have become less important in providing counterweights to official authority.

Another and equally fundamental cause for the declining significance of the adversary process as a restraint on excessive exertions of public authority is the abandonment of adversary procedures as the normal mode of determining criminal guilt in the United States. More than 90% of felony convictions are obtained on pleas of guilty,[39] and the resulting system is less one of guilt adjudication than of case processing and plea negotiation. Although present practices did not suddenly emerge in the current crises of American criminal justice,[40] there can be little doubt that much that occurred in the last generation has strongly influenced the historical trend. The inundation of the courts with prosecutions reinforces the perception that the great mass of criminal cases must be dealt with on a wholesale basis if the system is to function at all. But more is involved than merely numbers. The increasing severity of criminal penalties and other factors such as the thrust of federal sentencing guidelines have substantially enhanced the discretionary powers of prosecutors in the United States and have, in general, made decisions by the criminally accused to stand trial rather than to plead guilty more hazardous and less attractive.[41]

The system of plea bargaining in American criminal justice has received the benediction of the highest judicial authority.[42] Participants, including many members of the defense bar, appear, by and large, to accept and even approve the system of plea bargaining.[43] Nevertheless, there is incongruity in a system that encourages the barter of rights for leniency; to many it may be seen as denigrating the value of rights and trivializing the importance of punishment. Rule-of-law concerns abound. What emerges sharply from empirical studies of plea-bargaining practices is that the outcomes are governed very little by statute books or judicial opinions, not by preexisting law as contemplated by the *nulla poena* principle, but by policies created at the point of application.[44] The policies so expressed may often seek little more than administrative convenience and are often applied in ways that sacrifice the values of equality and uniformity. No effective movement to modify prevailing practices in any fundamental way yet appears in sight.[45]

It cannot be maintained that an adversary process conforming in all particulars to traditional American understandings is an absolute requisite to achieving the essential values of the rule of law. Other societies have pursued those objectives through institutional practices very different from our own, and with at least as great success. In many of the contrasting systems, elaborate arrangements for bureaucratic supervision and restraints have evolved, serving many of the objectives sought by adversary processes in the United States.[46] What seems to be occurring in this country is a considerable erosion of the adversary process as a regulatory instrumentality without, however, the development of anything approaching the compensating devices of centralized supervision characteristic of Western Europe.

II

It should not be understood that the weight of numbers afflicting American criminal justice is simply the product of increasing crime or that the flood of prosecutions and prisoners varies directly with the upward or downward movements of crime rates. We need not slight the significance of rampant criminality in the United States to appreciate that the dilemmas confronting almost every aspect of criminal justice are often as much the consequence of how the criminal inundation has been dealt with and the attitudes engendered by it as the consequence of the fact of crime itself. The phenomenon of prison overcrowding provides a useful illustration. As Franklin Zimring and Gordon Hawkins have demonstrated: "[v]ariations in crime do not help explain the peculiar pattern in prison rates in recent years."[47] In the decade 1972–1981, prison populations nearly doubled and that total more than doubled, between 1982 and 1992. Crime statistics indicate an increase in serious crime in the first of these decades but an overall decline in the second.[48] These variations in crime rates find no reflection in the steady upward progression of prison populations during the period. What is reflected are sentencing practices of great severity mandated by new legislation and sentencing guidelines, widespread judicial attitudes, and prosecution policies directed to unprecedented uses of penal incarceration. In Florida, where the burgeoning prison population forced adoption of an early-release program, 36% of the inmates (mostly drug offenders) were found ineligible for early release because they were incarcerated under mandatory minimum sentences. As a result, many prisoners who had been convicted of violent crimes, presumably prime candidates for continued incapacitation, were released, leaving in confinement many whose crimes included no elements of violence.[49] The issues associated with the extraordinary increases in prison population in American jurisdictions are among the most important confronting domestic policy. For present purposes they are additionally important because they demonstrate that the institutional environment in which the legality principle today is called on to function is the product not only of social and cultural forces giving rise to epidemics of crime but also of measures, attitudes, and emotions that the specter of criminality has called into being.[50]

The complexities and nuances of the present era of American criminal justice no doubt elude any simple formulation. Nevertheless, much can be learned by contemplating the ubiquitous phrases the "war on crime" and, particularly in the last decade and a half, the "war on drugs."[51] These locutions, of course, are political slogans calculated to rally public support for programs of governmental action and also for the political figures who propose and administer them. The slogans constitute important ingredients of the politics of crisis in these times. Cultivation of a sense of emergency and crisis has been a fundamental tactic of modern totalitarian regimes,[52] but the practice of crisis politics is no stranger to more liberal societies. In pluralistic communities, which by definition are composed of groups with widely differing interests and agendas, a sense of crisis engulfing the entire society may sometimes seem required to evoke sustained and serious response to important issues of public policy. Yet the costs of cultivating the atmosphere of emergency as a standard mode of political action are high for liberal societies. The costs may include the promoting of public attitudes that erode restraints on governmental power and produce misconceptions of the true nature of the problems addressed.[53]

Although the "war on crime," frequently invoked long before the present crisis in penal law enforcement emerged, is a political slogan, it is not wholly metaphoric. Even the United States Supreme Court has drawn an analogy between the war on drugs and a war against another nation and has suggested that, in both, the community interest may outweigh the individual's liberty interest.[54] The militaristic allusion is surprisingly literal in describing much that is being done in the name of crime control, as well as the psychology revealed both in public officials and in other members of the community during the last generation. The war on drugs, for example, has made direct use of the armed forces. In some jurisdictions the National Guard has been employed for drug-law enforcement in a variety of ways since 1977.[55]

More striking evidence of the militarization of law enforcement is to be found in the uses being made of the regular armed forces in the drug war. In 1981 the Posse Comitatus Act, which since the post–Civil War era has prohibited exercise by the military of police powers on the civilian population, was amended to mandate the armed forces' participation in drug-law enforcement.[56] That the departures from traditional inhibitions on use of the military in the administration of civilian justice have materially advanced the war on drugs may be in doubt, but the resulting redefinitions of the civilian and military spheres and of federal and state authority seem clear.

As in other wars, the war on drugs encounters problems of finance. It is said that in the years of the Bush administration, a period of budgetary constraint, $100 billion was expended on drug-control programs by federal, state, and local governments.[57] There has been a problem of armaments: in the many and violent street battles with illegal drug suppliers, the police are often outgunned, and a society fearful and outraged by crime has nevertheless appeared incapable of disarming its adversaries. The war on drugs has evolved a foreign policy. Other nations have been importuned to assist in cutting off supplies of narcotics produced for the American market. In the four years following 1989, some $2 billion was spent in an effort to destroy drug supplies at their sources in Peru, Colombia, and Bolivia.[58] The exigencies of drug-law enforcement on occasion may have corrupted the execution of American foreign policy. All but the merest hints of such contamination appear to have been studiously excluded from public view in the trial of the Panamanian satrap, Manuel Noriega.[59] Again, like other wars, the war on drugs has produced its quota of innocent victims. In a substantial number of instances, police raids, some of a violent nature, have been mistakenly directed against homes of innocent citizens, resulting in trauma and even death to the inhabitants.[60] The casualties of the war have been disproportionately high in minority communities, which have been victimized both by the drug traffic and by the measures employed to combat it.[61]

Declarations of war are portentous acts, not to be taken lightly,[62] which is true whether the enemies contemplated are external or internal, whether force is to be launched against foreign nations or members of one's own society. A war on crime or a war on drugs is a war on people. There can be no war without enemies, and defining adversaries as enemies may produce attitudes and measures that are difficult, if not sometimes impossible, to contain. For the larger part of a generation, we have found it easier to mount moral outrage over the spectacle of offenders escaping just deserts than over persons suffering excessive and unjust punishments by the state, although both phenomena have been in abundant evidence. Such attitudes—we may call them the war psychology—are not confined to the United States. A number of industrial nations, including Great Britain,[63] Israel,[64] and the Republic of Ireland,[65] facing seemingly uncontrollable escalations of crime and terrorism, have adapted their legal institutions to conform more closely to what Sir Leon Radzinowicz has described as authoritarian models of criminal justice.[66] These are systems emphasizing a more unrestrained exercise of the public force, enhanced discretion of official agents, and increasing insensitivity to the rights and immunities of persons caught up in the criminal process. The movement has, in short, been one toward the weakening of the legality principle and the accompanying institutional habits of legality.

Over two centuries ago Voltaire warned that "where charity is wanting, law is always cruel."[67] Charity has not been the salient characteristic of American penal policy during the last generation. The period has been distinguished by a revival of the death penalty, increased utilization of penal incarceration, and dwindling rehabilitative aspirations and opportunities within the correctional system. The approach taken to the problems of drug use and addiction has been overwhelmingly punitive in nature.[68] Even medical uses of marijuana and needle-exchange programs have been opposed, not primarily because of any supposed inefficacy as therapeutic or public health measures, but rather because any officially tolerated uses of narcotics are seen as weakening the deterrent thrust of national drug policy.[69] The war against crime has not only eschewed charity as a leading characteristic, it has also discouraged serious thought about the causes of burgeoning crime in American society and what it may have to say about needs for social reconstruction. If we are fighting a war on crime, then criminals are enemies; and the characterization inhibits consideration of our own responsibilities for conditions that may breed and encourage criminal behavior. The soldier in the front line is rarely a social reformer.

The war on drugs has contributed importantly to the environment in which the rule of law functions today. Any rational appraisal of the war on drugs as it has emerged in the last decade and a half must focus in large measure on the costs of present drug policy. One category of costs largely neglected in modern political discourse is that resulting in debilitation of the legality ideal and weakening of the habits of legality. The costs are substantial, and their consequences extend to areas of American social and political life far removed from drug-law enforcement.

The war on drugs has taken on for many the attributes of a moral crusade.[70] To understand why such effort and sincerity result in serious assaults on the values of legality, it is necessary to appreciate the enormous difficulties of achieving the objectives of the drug warriors. The goal of American drug policy was officially stated in the Anti-Drug Abuse Act of 1988 to be the creation of "A Drug-Free America by 1995."[71] The acceptance of objectives so far removed from possible realization breeds resort to desperate and illusory remedies and gives point to the statement of an American police chief: "We are all trapped into the language of 'a war on drugs.'"[72] Current drug policy proposes to prevent the sale of drugs in certain categories for which there is strong and persistent demand. Unlike many other forms of serious criminality, the victims of the illegal drug traffic are willing victims, unlikely to cooperate in drug law enforcement. Attempts to prevent sales to such purchasers must of necessity frequently involve intrusion by public agents into the most intimate precincts of private life. The illegal market resulting from drug prohibitions offers wealth beyond the dreams of avarice to large operators both in and out of the country and opportunities for financial gain lacking in legitimate pursuits for many members of the minority community.

Problems of interdicting supplies of drugs originating outside the national boundaries, as in the Prohibition era, have proved formidable and probably insuperable.[73]

American drug policy has obstructed the practice of legality in multifarious ways, only a few of which can be sketched here. It is difficult to conceive of a more direct and devastating subversion of the rule of law than that resulting from the literal corruption of law enforcement personnel. Yet the staggering amounts of money generated by the illegal drug traffic create opportunities for theft by and bribery of federal and state police agents, and inevitably some have succumbed to the unprecedented temptations. Because the behavior is sub rosa, quantitative estimates of how far such corruption has proceeded are necessarily tentative. It is reasonable to infer, however, that such episodes as the alleged theft of drug funds and money laundering by FBI and U.S. Customs personnel reported in 1993[74] and the revelations of rampant corruption in some divisions of the New York Police Department in the same year[75] indice much more extensive pathologies not yet fully exposed. Police corruption, of course, preceded the current war on drugs and will no doubt persist after present policies subside. Yet it is doubtful that in this century inducements to gross corruption have been greater than at present. Only the Prohibition era, which resembles the present in this respect and many others, provided comparable dangers to the morale and integrity of American criminal justice.[76]

It is characteristic of wars and other periods of emergency that restraints on the discretion of public officers are relaxed and that public powers are expanded at the expense of private rights and individual immunities. The extensive resort to undercover agents in drug-law enforcement epitomizes both tendencies.[77] The undercover agent, who may be either a member of a police organization or a private individual, sometimes with an extensive record of prior criminal violations, exercises a broad discretion that by the nature of his or her role must often be largely unsupervised by administrative superiors. The agent acts in many instances without accountability: criminal acts committed by the agent in the course of his or her duties may be undiscovered or ignored, or punishments may be withheld or mitigated.[78] Perjury, entrapment, and gross intrusions into areas of personal privacy have always been associated with the police spy and the agent provocateur.[79] Yet with full awareness of the chronic abuses associated with such instrumentalities, American courts have consistently defended the undercover system against effective constitutional attack and have done so with the apparent conviction that, without resort to the undercover agent, enforcement of drug laws and other legislation requiring comparable intrusions on privacy may often be impossible.[80] The assumption of the courts indeed may be correct, and the toleration of unsupervised discretion and of diminished accountability of public agents thus becomes one of the significant costs enhanced by current penal policy.

The exigencies of drug-law enforcement have provided powerful motivations in the ongoing erosion of constitutional protections against abuse by public agents in the administration of criminal justice. In recent years the Supreme Court has significantly restated the law of the Fourth Amendment. Not only has the exclusionary rule been drastically weakened, the substantive rights encompassed by the amendment have also been severely constricted.[81] No doubt the phenomena reflect, in part, judicial empathy for law enforcement personnel confronted by dangerous and sometimes apparently impossible demands and deference to the policy directives of other branches of the government. The posture perhaps underlies the Court's remarkable 1992 decision that the kidnapping of a Mexican citizen in his home country by American agents and transporting him to the United States to stand trial did not offend the provisions of the extradition treaty between the two countries, because the text did not specifically deal with the subject of kidnapping.[82] What may not often have been noted is that the current tendencies of the Court result not only in the diminishment of constitutional rights, but also in a contraction of the rule of law, for in many areas the only relevant law has been the Fourth Amendment.[83] With the elimination of constitutional constraints, the police are often relegated to the undefined preserves of "reasonableness," unencumbered and unguided by meaningful norms. The inclination of the modern Court to accommodate its jurisprudence to the per-

ceived requirements of law enforcement in a difficult era
has not gone without protest from some of its members. On
one occasion Justice Thurgood Marshall, in dissent, noted
that there is "no drug exception in the Constitution."[84] If,
indeed, the Court's readings of Bill of Rights restraints could
be restricted to cases involving drug sale or use, the dangers
of the new constitutional law would be less formidable. But
experience both in this country and abroad confirms the
truth that relaxations of basic restraints on official power are
rarely confined to the situations of emergency that gave rise
to them. Instead, the resulting losses of control over the machinery of criminal justice extend to the broader functioning
of the system, into areas in which different and less pressing
urgencies exist.[85]

The modern war on drugs suggests certain historical
analogies. In mid-eighteenth century England, for example,
the government was confronted by rampant criminality, in
both the cities and the countryside, but was armed with an
enforcement mechanism wholly inadequate to prevent the
commission of offenses or to apprehend more than an insig-
nificant fraction of serious offenders.[86] The official reaction
to the crime epidemic and to the fears and frustrations engendered by it included the administration of a deterrent
regime described by the novelist Samuel Richardson, with
apparent approval, as "Terror-menaced Punishment."[87] In
an effort to compensate for the absence of an effective
crime-prevention strategy directed against the many, penalties of extraordinary harshness were inflicted on the offenders who could be apprehended and convicted. Well over
200 offenses were made punishable by the death penalty,
covering a spectrum ranging from the most serious to the
trivial.[88]The gibbet became a central motif of the times. The
war on crime in eighteenth-century England, like that in late
twentieth-century America, numbered among its victims the
principle of penal proportion.

During the past two and a half centuries, a persistent
strand in liberal thought relating to penal justice has been
the notion that the severity of criminal penalties should be
limited by and proportioned to the culpability of the offender
and his offense.[89] In the United States the concept of penal
proportion has even found its way into constitutional doc-

trine, notably that concerned with prohibitions against cruel and unusual punishment.[90] It is an idea notoriously difficult of definition and application: the meaning of culpability and the measurement of its degree elude mathematical precision and therefore produce controversy and conflict. Yet the competing considerations of deterrence and certainly those of penal rehabilitationism are beset by perhaps even greater awkwardness of definition and practical application. Knowledge of when sanctions deter and at what levels of severity optimum prevention can be effected is often lacking.[91] Even the goals of rehabilitative efforts may be ambiguous, and the means to secure them are typically inadequate or lacking.[92] The continuing importance of the concept of proportionality, despite obscurities of meaning and application, may be confirmed by imagining a society subject to a penal regime in which the lawmaking authority and the courts are at liberty to impose sanctions of great severity in total disregard of the degrees of culpability revealed by offenders. Even if such a regime could be made to operate at all, the costs in human dignity and justice would be prohibitive.

The intensity of the assault on the proportionality principle by the current war on drugs does not approach that in the society just imagined. Yet modern drug legislation is distinguished by its small concerns for gradations in the culpability of offenders and the relative dangerousness of their crimes. Nor has significant interest been revealed in the comparative seriousness of drug offenses and other types of criminal behavior, with the result that the entire corpus of criminal legislation, when viewed as a whole, has become increasingly incoherent. The nature of modern drug legislation no doubt reflects a strong conviction in the community of the dangers attendant on drug use and sale.[93] But the advocacy of such measures has rarely revealed thoughtful efforts to balance culpability and sanctions, and there is little evidence of anything approaching sober proportionality analysis in policies like that of "no tolerance," avidly advanced by administrative spokespersons in the 1980s. Instead, such postures displayed a determined disregard of all competing considerations in the efforts to secure all-important deterrent and incapacitative objectives. The federal sentencing guidelines by eliminating many traditional principles of leniency in the sentencing process often reinforce a criminal jurisprudence that increasingly disregards the proportionality principle.[94] Penalties for drug offenses have been enhanced to the point of authorizing the death penalty in certain situations.[95] Mandatory minimum terms of imprisonment have exacerbated problems of prison overcrowding and, more relevantly to the purposes at hand, resulted in capricious allocations of penal restraints among offending members of the population.[96] There has been a striking increase in the uses of property forfeiture as an instrument of drug-law enforcement at both federal and state levels.[97] Forfeiture, often administered with only minimal protections afforded affected parties, has frequently resulted in draconian sanctions being imposed on persons whose conduct was of small seriousness and sometimes on innocent third parties.[98] By their nature, the incidence and scope of forfeiture are determined primarily, not by gradations in the culpability of offenders, but rather by the presence or absence of property that may be made subject to seizure.

It may be objected that the principle of penal proportion, relating as it does to the substantive content of the law rather than to any of its formal aspects, bears no relation to the rule-of-law concept.[99] Thus, it can be argued that legislation authorizing sanctions grossly disproportionate to the culpability of accused persons, however unjust and dubious as a matter of penal policy, does not offend the legality ideal so long as the law is clearly articulated and consistently applied to those who violate its provisions. Yet excluding the proportionality principle from the definition of the rule-of-law concept does not preclude recognition that penal proportion, when recognized and applied, enhances the likelihood that the legality principle will be afforded significant expression within the system of criminal justice or that ignoring penal proportion gives rise to genuine rule-of-law concerns. That the principle of penal proportion contributes to a fuller realization of the rule of law is strongly suggested by the intimate association of the two concepts throughout their modern history. It seems no accident that Beccaria, the great exponent of rule-of-law values in criminal justice administration, was also the first modern writer to articulate a comprehensive case for penal proportion.[100]

The insouciance toward the proportionality principle manifested in the war on drugs weakens legality values in a variety of ways. Experience with the Rockefeller law in New York, among the most punitive drug statutes so far enacted in the states, is illustrative. Provisions in the New York law providing mandatory punishments of 15 to 25 years' imprisonment for possession of narcotics discourages defendants from challenging the state in court.[101] There is evidence that a number of female drug couriers in New York commit acts of possession under private threats of violence or other forms of duress, a defense that might sometimes prevail if adequately presented in court.[102] But the combination of ignorance, poverty, and the concomitant absence of adequate legal services, on the one hand, and the threat of draconian penalties if the defense fails, on the other, produces great leverage on the accused to plea bargain and concede guilt to lesser offenses. Thus the congruence of the law's principles and their application, identified by Professor Lon Fuller as an essential attribute of the legality ideal, is weakened or destroyed.[103]

In the twentieth century, as in the eighteenth, disregard of the proportionality principle, which relates the severity of penalties to the culpability of the accused, may result in the phenomenon of nullification.[104] Nullification occurs when the penalties mandated by the law appear grossly inappropriate to at least some of those persons responsible for the law's administration. At such times, functionaries—police, prosecutors, jurors, or judges—may resist the law's commands and obstruct their application. Despite the intensity of support gained for the modern war on drugs, evidences of the nullification phenomenon in drug-law enforcement are not lacking. Adverse reactions of official personnel to certain aspects of penal drug policy may reflect a sense of moral incongruity or a purpose to relieve the system of part of the weight of numbers created by disproportionate sentences. In some instances judicial resistance to the provisions of drug legislation has been candid and overt, as in the case of a Michigan judge who flatly refused to apply statutory penalties he deemed unconscionable in the circumstances of the particular prosecution.[105] More recently, a senior federal district judge removed himself from trying minor drug cases because, he said, "of mandated and unnecessarily harsh sentences for minor drug offenders, which fail to deter."[106] It is reported that in some federal districts, prosecutors decline marijuana cases involving less than a ton, while in others severe penalties are imposed on persons cultivating a few plants for their own use.[107] Practices of nullification signal a dissonance in the operation of the legal order, a clash of values and purposes. Evidences of such resistance are perhaps not wholly to be regretted, for they may presage a more favorable environment for reconsidering basic attitudes that have dominated the American war on drugs. Yet nullification, if prolonged and intense, is antagonistic to the rule of law and the habits of legality. It pits officials against the mandates of the law, and its effect on those caught up in the system is unequal and capricious and hence inequitable.

That efforts to minimize the sale and use of narcotic drugs will remain an important responsibility of the American system of criminal justice for the indefinite future can hardly be doubted. Franklin Zimring and Gordon Hawkins, writing in the early 1990s, observed that "[p]ublic support for extreme governmental response to drugs is higher than for authoritarian countermeasures to any other social problem."[108] It is too early to revise the statement, but certain developments provide what may be faint evidences of an increasing willingness to subject at least certain aspects of American drug policy to a more rational public discourse.[109] One of these is the genuine concern expressed by some members of the judiciary about prevailing law governing the sentencing of drug offenders, both because of its harsh and disproportionate treatment of many minor offenders who are more victims of the drug trade than criminals, and because of its distorting effect on the uses of limited prison resources. Another such evidence may be the long-delayed response of the Supreme Court to glaring deficiencies in the procedures of property forfeiture in drug cases and in the ruling that disproportions between the culpability of the owner and the value of the property seized may be so great as to offend constitutional limitations.[110] These are hardly impressive auguries, and not all that has occurred in the recent past points in the same direction. Yet the costs of the current war on drugs, measured in money or in institutional or human terms, are great; and time for dispassionate auditing of the costs is overdue.

In the last decade and a half, persons seeking a rational reappraisal of American drug policy have sometimes been subjected to public ridicule and political reprisals with repressive consequences not unlike those arising from wartime restraints on free speech. Yet the costs of the war on drugs as conducted in the recent past, whether calculated in money, social fragmentation, or the weakening of basic political values, strongly counsel the importance and urgency of reconsideration. Sober realism supports the search for a policy located at some point between a wholly unregulated legalization of the sale and use of drugs like heroin and cocaine, on the one hand, and the continuation of an internecine civil war, on the other. Not the least-important gains to be anticipated from a successful implementation of such a posture would be the opportunity to rejuvenate and enlarge the institutional habits of legality in American society.

III

No portrayal of the environment of legality in the generation just past can ignore the role of the death penalty in the United States. It is a complex phenomenon and one that can be given only cursory attention in these remarks. That the present high levels of support for capital punishment in American society are in significant part a product of fears and outrage engendered by perceptions of epidemic criminality and that the death penalty performs a significant symbolic function in the aggregation of attitudes, measures, and practices constituting the "war on crime" are observations not likely to be seriously contested. Indeed, the growth in popular support for capital punishment and the decline of the rehabilitative ideal in American corrections constitute two of the most striking movements of opinion in the era under consideration and must surely reflect common sources.[111] In 1966, at the very beginning of the present era, public-opinion polls recorded for the first time a larger support for abolishing than for retaining capital punishment. Yet by 1981 a Gallup poll reported two-thirds of the population in support of the death penalty. More recent polls reveal considerably higher levels of support and the corresponding weakening of abolitionist sentiment.[112] To be sure, the results of public-opinion polling may indicate a less monolithic support for capital punishment when the questions posed are formulated in differing ways.[113] Nor can it be safely assumed that the public desires or would tolerate the precipitate execution of all the more than 2,700 persons currently on death row in the United States.[114] Nevertheless, the emergence of the death penalty as a widely accepted symbol of the struggle against rampant criminality in American society is one of the unmistakable realities of the times.

Viewed from an international perspective, the revival and expansion of the death penalty in the United States since the 1960s is a striking anomaly. Capital punishment has been abandoned in virtually all other industrial states. After the fall of the Iron Curtain, many of the Eastern Europe societies, as a matter of national priority, have moved to abolish capital punishment. "[E]xecution as an instrumentality of state power," it is said, "has become almost exclusively a Third World phenomenon, practiced with enthusiasm only in Moslem states, in China and parts of Africa."[115]

Explanation of the unique posture of the United States toward the death penalty among the democratic nations of the world requires more than simple reference to American statistics of violent crime. Other industrial societies in recent years have also experienced high levels of violence and terrorism that produce insecurity and outrage in the affected populations, but they have, nevertheless, rejected efforts to restore executions as part of their policies of social defense.[116] The differences in attitudes toward the death penalty in the United States may be explained in part by historical antecedents. In the nineteenth century, leadership of the abolition movement in the continental countries came in significant part from working-class groups and political parties of the left, moved by memories of authoritarian regimes that employed the death penalty as an instrument of oppression.[117] In the United States, where memories of political oppression were perhaps less vivid, abolition sentiment was expressed largely in the educated middle classes who tended to view abolition of the death penalty less as an escape from tyranny than as an opportunity to establish a more humane penal regime with strong rehabilitative overtones.[118] Today, in Eastern Europe and in developing countries seeking to establish democratic institutions, elimination of the death penalty is seen as an essential first step toward a regime of human rights and the rule of law.[119] Fears of capital punishment as an instrumentality of authoritarian government, however, have played little part in the death-penalty debate in the United States; the concern that undergirds support for capital punishment is, rather, the fear of widespread and violent crime. The notion that the death penalty enhances the potential for authoritarian rule in this country, if advanced, would likely be rejected by most Americans as fanciful and academic.

The capital punishment regime that has emerged in the United States since the decision of *Gregg v. Georgia*[120] in 1976 presents an array of oddities and ambiguities. In recent years, about 2 of 100 persons convicted of murder are sentenced to death. About 250 new residents on death row are added each year, but only about 10% of that number are executed each year.[121] Inevitably, the population of death rows has steadily and rapidly enlarged. By far, the greater number of executions has occurred in the southern states.[122] Whether the meager rate of executions will persist in other states recognizing the death penalty as in California, whose death row population is now the largest in the country, and whether public opinion will support a greatly increased number of executions in the country as a whole are obviously questions of some moment.[123]

The practices surrounding the death penalty that have become established since the *Gregg* decision are in many respects remarkably harsh. There is little evidence of an "etiquette of capital punishment" of the sort displayed in Great Britain before the abolition of the death penalty in that country, which generally resulted in the withholding of executions in cases in which serious doubts about the appropriateness of the sanction had been expressed by official personnel in the course of adjudication.[124] In the United States, death sentences are regularly upheld by narrowly divided courts;[125] the Supreme Court has approved of state legislation authorizing sentencing judges to depart from jury recommendations of mercy;[126] the role of executive clemency in death cases, responding to public outcry and political pressures, has been diminished to near insignificance.[127] The attitudes engendered in the present crisis of public order have resulted in severe limitations on the application of the insanity defense in criminal litigation.[128] Persons reading any considerable number of appellate decisions reviewing death sentences may well conclude that a latent function of the death penalty as administered in states where executions are frequent is to rid the community of its violently disturbed or mentally deficient members.[129] Both the International Covenant of Civil and Political Rights and the American Covenant of Human Rights would withhold the death penalty from crimes perpetrated by offenders below the age of 18.[130] In 1989 the Supreme Court upheld a sentence of death imposed on an offender who was 16 at the time of the murder.[131]

Constructing the current regime of capital punishment has exacted great costs and imposed heavy burdens on the judicial systems of both state and federal governments. Death-penalty prosecutions are expensive of time and effort and contribute significantly to the current problems created by overburdened dockets of civil and criminal cases. It is said that about a half of the death sentences are reversed on initial appeal.[132] The extraordinary efforts of appellate judges, particularly in state courts, to regularize the administration of capital punishment during the last two decades must constitute a significant fraction of the judicial labors in those courts. The posture of the Supreme Court toward its role in capital cases has strikingly altered with the passage of time.[133] In the 1976 case of *Woodson v. North Carolina* the Court remarked: "[T]he penalty of death is qualitatively different from a sentence of imprisonment. . . . [T]here is a corresponding difference in the need for reliability in the determination that death is the appropriate punishment in a specific case."[134] The Court thus appeared to found its own approach to capital cases on an acute appreciation of the seriousness of the issues presented and the evident uniqueness of the death penalty. Following the *Gregg* case, the Court was deeply engaged in efforts to establish a system of "guided discretion" in state death cases. In the 1980s, however, the Court's determination to distance and disengage itself from the administration of capital punishment in the states became increasingly clear. The purpose was demonstrated in a variety of forms, including the imposition of stringent restrictions on the habeas corpus remedy in capital cases,[135] the tolerance of state exclusion from trial juries of those expressing reservations about the death penalty,[136] and the resort to the device of "harmless error" in upholding the validity of state proceedings.[137] So strong and precipitate have been the Court's efforts at disengagement that at times it has appeared to promote rather than to monitor the death penalty.

The apparent willingness of the Court to distance itself from the administration of capital punishment, even at the expense of values deemed of overriding importance as recently as two decades ago, invites speculation. It may be thought that certain members of the Court are simply reflecting the zeitgeist of the times. Some commentators point to what may be called a fear of contamination, a concern that continued close association of the federal courts with the administration of capital punishment in the states endangers their prestige and authority by identifying them as primary sources of delay in justice and by involving them in acrimonious criticism and controversy.[138] Overriding other considerations, however, is the concern of the Court that close monitoring of the death penalty in the states constitutes an unreasonable drain on the Court's time and energy and menaces its capacity to deal adequately with other issues presented to it of greater interest to the Court and of larger importance to the country. This concern is surely proper and inevitable and by no means peculiar to the present majority justices. Yet the modern impulse of the Court to distance itself from the realities of capital punishment administration has been immoderate, and I suspect that it will ultimately fail in its purpose. The policy of abstention denies the essence of what the Court has done for more than 60 years to protect Fourteenth Amendment rights of persons confronted by the power of the state in the criminal process. Indeed, it was in the capital cases that the Court was first drawn to apply the federal mandates of due process and equal protection of the laws to state criminal proceedings.[139]

Then as now, the death penalty implicated the most basic of human rights. Unhappily, vindication of those rights in many instances still demands federal judicial intervention; and this reality may well force the reluctant attention of the Court as long as the constitutional validity of the death penalty is proclaimed.

It is not the purpose of these remarks to debate the abolition of the death penalty. It is, rather, to inquire whether in contemporary America sound habits of legality characterize the performance of the most drastic and somber of governmental functions, the execution of offenders. Scrutiny of actual institutional practices surrounding the administration of capital punishment has led many persons to conclude that the process is pervaded by a kind of inherent lawlessness. Amnesty International, no friend of the death penalty, asserts: "No means of limiting the death penalty can prevent its being imposed arbitrarily or unfairly."[140]

Ironically, it was principally rule-of-law concerns that first led the Supreme Court to assume an active role in death-penalty litigation, a perception that in earlier decades the selection of offenders for execution, at best, was made capriciously and, at worst, was influenced by bias and discrimination.[141] The Court responded by insisting that before the death penalty is imposed, the circumstances of the particular case must be examined and that the ultimate issue of death or imprisonment should be guided by legislatively articulated norms and guidelines. A large majority of state legislatures responded with alacrity and enacted statutes that were thought to comply with the new constitutional demands. Typically, the new statutes identified considerations of aggravation and mitigation and sought to distinguish capital from noncapital killings by the use of such terms as "heinous" and "cruel." It cannot be doubted that the present edifice of law and practice is the product of great and often conscientious efforts. It is clear, also, that many of those offenders on whom capital sentences have been imposed would have been selected for death under any regime of capital punishment. Yet the statutory formulas are required to bear extraordinary weight. In only 2 of 100 convictions for murder in the United States are sentences of death imposed.[142] Inevitably, doubts arise about the capacity of the verbal devices being employed to separate from the mass of murder convictions those cases meriting the extreme penalty, consistently with the demands of rationality and equity. "To define in advance the elements that make some killings more worthy of punishment than others is difficult," it has been asserted, "but to define criteria for choosing one case in 100 or 200 is impossible."[143] Study of extended sequences of death-penalty adjudication does little to inspire confidence in the fairness or rationality of the systems that have emerged. In some instances the Supreme Court, moved perhaps by an overriding urge to routinize capital punishment administration, quickly approved state legislation and practices that, in fact, do little either to guide or constrict discretion in death-penalty decision making.[144] In other state jurisdictions, the calculus of heinousness, or what Justice Byron White referred to as the "fine tuning calibration of depravity," has not produced coherence in the selection of offenders for the extreme penalty.[145]

The basic causes of the failure to eliminate caprice from the administration of capital punishment, however, do not reside alone in deficiencies in state statutes governing the standards and procedures of death-penalty sentencing. Sentencing statutes do not cure the effects of rampant, unregulated discretion pervading the process from its earliest stages; and sentencing laws alone, however expertly crafted, can contribute comparatively little to the objective of a system satisfying the requisites of the legality ideal. At the outset of the process, prosecutorial decisions must be made whether to seek a death sentence or to plea-bargain and accept sentences of imprisonment. These are decisions ordinarily guided by no official guidelines, vulnerable to political pressures and community biases, subject to little or nothing by way of administrative or judicial supervision, and largely ignored by the Court's constitutional canon. It may come as a surprise to learn that prosecutorial decisions to pursue the death penalty are often influenced by the state of local public finance. In many jurisdictions, costs of felony prosecutions are borne not by the state but by county governments, and the expenditures incurred in prosecuting death cases may place substantial strains on local resources.[146] It may be inferred, therefore, that to an indeterminate and varying de-

gree, the peril of capital punishment encountered by offenders is a function of where they are tried and of the fiscal
resources available to county prosecutors. That the various
factors weighing on prosecutorial decisions to invoke death
sentences are productive of caprice and incoherence may be
sufficiently indicated by noting differences in the frequency
with which decisions to seek death are made by prosecutors
in different parts of the country, in different regions within
the same state jurisdiction, and in the same prosecutorial
offices over time.[147] Once the judicial process is com-
menced, it often falls far below acceptable standards. Virtually all death-penalty defendants are indigent, and the failure of the states to provide adequate legal representation for
the accused, both at trial and on appeal, has insufficiently
taxed the conscience of the public and its officers.[148]

It has been typical of the Court's interventions in the
administration of criminal justice to neglect or ignore the relations of particular problems under consideration to the
operation of the system as a whole. Efforts of counsel and
commentators to supply factual data describing those relations have not been greeted by the Court with notable enthusiasm. As early as the *Gregg* case, the role of unregulated
prosecutorial discretion in death-penalty cases was brought
to the Court's attention. Justice Byron White, in an opinion
for himself and two other members of the Court, responded,
first, by objecting that the argument that prosecutors "be-
have in a standardless fashion in deciding which cases to try
as capital felonies is unsupported by any facts."[149] That the
Justices were unwilling to treat the proposition as a proper
subject of judicial notice is hardly surprising. Yet with the
advantage of hindsight, we must doubt that the position of
the Court would have been significantly affected had carefully collected and organized data been submitted to support
the proposition. In later cases the stance of the Court has
been to express an impatient skepticism of such data and
ultimately to conclude that, even if valid, the facts could not
alter the outcome of the litigation. The most notable, but by
no means the only, example of the tendency is the 1987 case
of *McCleskey v. Kemp,* in which the Court announced the
constitutional irrelevance of a demonstrated systemic bias

toward the imposition of the death penalty in cases of white, as contrasted to black, victims.[150]

Perhaps more disquieting is Justice White's further statement in the *Gregg* opinion that "Petitioner's argument that there is an unconstitutional amount of discretion in the system which separates those suspects who receive the death penalty and those who receive life imprisonment . . . seems to be in final analysis an indictment of our entire system of justice."[151] To some, the statement may appear to anathematize arguments based on inquiry into the operating realities of the death penalty, on the ground that entertaining such issues endangers the entire structure of the American criminal justice system. If this reading is accurate, the statement expresses a great and, it is hoped, unjustified pessimism that the Court can operate in these areas only by turning its head away from reality. Justice White appears to say that prosecutorial discretion operates as a significant factor not only in the death-penalty cases but also more generally throughout the system, which is clearly correct. But if the statement suggests that the resulting problems are the same or of comparable magnitude in the death cases as in others, it is incorrect. The pyramiding of unregulated or inadequately regulated discretion in cases leading to executions, the fiscal factors, the history and recollections of discrimination, the difficulties encountered in defending basic rights at trial, the potency of emotions engendered, and the dangers of social polarization and fragmentation in some applications of capital punishment and its irrevocable consequences combine to demonstrate the correctness of the Court when it first perceived the uniqueness of the death penalty.

If certainty, predictability, equality in the application of extreme state power, and official decisions made subject to articulate legal norms are essential constituents of the rule of law, then the administration of capital punishment in the United States must be found seriously wanting. Thus at the point at which the state is imposing its most stringent sanctions, at the point where the need is greatest for the constraints of legality to be of surest application, the habits of legality are found to be weak and ineffectual.

For almost three decades American society has faced a crisis of criminality and public disorder. The insecurities engendered have, naturally enough, bred fear and outrage; and these emotions, sometimes carefully cultivated by political strategists, underlie much of the penal policy that has evolved in these times. Outrage breeds a climate threatening to the values of legality. Jeremy Bentham wrote, "*Fear* is a *passion* by which judgment is laid prostrate and carried away captive."[152] Yet fear and insecurity are inevitable reactions to rampant criminality, and little is gained by simply deploring them. What is required are voices raised to assert the importance of preserving the basic political values in a time of troubles and demonstrations that rationality of public response, which is advanced by the rule of law, often promotes, rather than weakens, personal security. For a decade and a half, such voices in the public forum have been few and weak. It is a matter of high importance that they be strengthened.

Not all problems obstructing realization of the legality ideal in American criminal justice, however, are products of recent crises. The structure of American political institutions and practices that have grown up around them present continuing difficulties in maintaining and enlarging the habits of legality. These problems supply the focus of the next chapter.

3

The Structural Impediments
to Legality

A political society governed by the rule of law is one in which exercises of public authority are guided by articulate legal norms and in which public officers are held to high standards of accountability. No society succeeds in giving full expression to the legality ideal, and departures from it may result from a great number of distinct influences. As discussed in the second chapter, a widespread perception that vital community or personal interests are being threatened by crime, terrorism, international aggression, or other menaces may cause public officers to act beyond the authorizations of existing law or to seek new laws that weaken the officers' accountability;[1] and they do so often with the approval, or even at the insistence, of a democratic majority.[2] We in the United States have been living in such a period for more than a generation. But there are other factors of history, tradition, and institutional structure that may exert more persistent and equally potent influences limiting realization of the legality ideal. It is probably impossible to separate the impacts of history and structure, for they are often inextricably intertwined. The structure of institutions generates habits and traditions, while historical attitudes, in turn, are among the determinants of institutional structure and its subsequent modifications.

If asked to identify the most distinctive aspect of American criminal justice, a foreign visitor familiar with the institutions of continental Europe, Japan, or even Great Britain would likely identify the extraordinary decentralization—or fragmentation—of the American system. In the United States, of course, there is no single official or agency politically responsible for the effectiveness and decency of criminal justice administration as a whole. There is no national ministry of justice nor even a home office.[3] The radical decentralization of the various institutional elements is not simply a product of federalism but also persists within the federal establishment, within the states, and at the local levels. A large metropolitan area may be policed by more than 100 separate law enforcement units, none of which is under effective legal constraint to coordinate its efforts with other similar agencies.[4] Prosecutors typically operate free of meaningful supervision by superior administrative authority.[5] Coordination of the efforts of local police and prosecuting agencies with those of county, state, or federal governmental bodies is generally rudimentary, informal, and uncompelled by law. The traditions of localism find strong expression in the American courts. Appellate review of lower-court decisions does not wholly overcome the realities of local judicial autonomy. Unlike the practices of judges in other societies, such as Japan, the American judge serves his or her tenure largely in the same judicial district and is spared a variety of intrusions of administrative oversight typical of many foreign systems.[6] Despite the modern efforts in many American jurisdictions to achieve centralized judicial administration, the attitudes of localism remain strong and sometimes obdurate.[7]

While largely free of the formal constraints integral to systems of criminal justice in other industrialized nations, the operation of individual units charged with functions of criminal justice in the United States is affected and conditioned by the practices of other units performing similar or related functions. Decisions made at one stage of the criminal process profoundly affect what is or can be done at other stages. A decision by a police department not to enforce a category of criminal legislation, as that relating to gambling, constricts prosecutorial options when, as is most often the case, the prosecutor depends on the police to apprehend offenders and bring them into court. So also, a disposition of judges to dismiss certain sorts of prosecutions against juvenile offenders or those charged with prostitution, for example, will often determine what police and prosecutors do when confronted by such behavior. That the operations at any level of criminal justice affect those at all other levels in ways both obvious and unexpected is one of the insights most necessary to understanding the functioning of criminal justice institutions, either at home or abroad.[8] But mutuality of effect among discrete administrative units does not produce an integrated system of criminal justice, nor does it result in coherent or comprehensive criminal policies. On the contrary, the effects are often capricious and uncalculated and unknown and unsuspected even by the persons or agencies producing them.

It is not surprising to discover that in such a loosely coupled system,[9] informal patterns of cooperation and coordination emerge independently of legal compulsion. Such patterns may reflect a conviction on the part of the participating agencies that cooperation serves their own best interests. At other times efforts at coordination may result from public or media pressures. One of the factors determining the forms and strength of such interaction is the degree to which political power is centralized in the community. Strong machine rule may result in viable, if sub rosa, patterns of cooperation among the various criminal justice bodies. The patterns may become weaker and less distinct when, as has been generally true in recent years, centralized control in large cities erodes or disappears.[10] As would be expected, the impulse toward larger coordination of law enforcement efforts has been particularly evident in such areas as drug-law enforcement and the control of terrorist activity.[11] Yet intergovernmental and interagency initiatives are attended by difficulties arising from the prevailing fragmentation of function and authority. Some local agencies simply opt out of federally inspired operations.[12] Local apathy or resistance appears to have obstructed enforcement of federal hate-crime legislation.[13] Even within the federal establishment, interagency task forces formed to combat organized crime often achieve small success.[14] At the local level, informal modes of coordination and information sharing are limited in their applications and operate sporadically. In his 1975 study of the Chicago police department, Kenneth Culp Davis found that conferences on law enforcement policy between prosecutors and high-ranking police officials rarely took place and that patrol officers' understanding of prosecutors' attitudes and practices was highly deficient.[15]

The fragmentation of American criminal justice and the traditions of localism that surround the functioning of the system's multiple individual units breed large consequences for its effectiveness and accountability. It is a system, at the outset, highly parochial in its attitudes and strongly resistant to reform. Radical decentralization in the area of policing and prosecution weakens the accountability of public officers for the uses made of the public force. The very number of individual and largely autonomous units and the low public visibility of many crucial decisions made by them render effective public monitoring of official performance difficult and often impossible. The traditions of localism, at the same time, prevent or obstruct achievement of effective routine administrative oversight, especially those forms of scrutiny that are external to the operating agencies.

The concerns engendered by the radical decentralization of authority in the American system extend beyond the specter of undetected abuses of the rights of persons caught up in the criminal process but include, also, the limitations the system imposes on the formulation of coherent penal policies and on the capacities of the system to achieve its basic utilitarian objectives. Viewed broadly, the central issue of American criminal justice administration is not whether discretionary decisions will be made by officials operating within the system, for the nature of the myriad problems that confront it make such decisions inescapable. The more pertinent questions are, Does the system articulate and enforce norms for the guidance of discretion when it is exercised? and Whose discretion will ultimately determine the policies and consequences of official action in the penal area? The locus of discretion is of critical importance, for the possibilities of both the rationality and effectiveness of penal policy may rest on its proper placement.[16] Typically in American practice, penal policy emerges from no central agency devoted to the achievement of broad policy objectives but is, instead, the product of hundreds of discretionary decisions made by officials in individual cases, decision makers who are not primarily concerned with or aware of the effects of their determinations on the achievement of rational policy overall.

Examples of conflicting purposes and measures arising from misallocations of governing discretionary authority are not difficult to summon. A state wishing to accord greater importance to the public health aspects of drug abuse than that supplied by the national war on drugs may find its efforts weakened or frustrated by decisions of federal law enforcement officials operating in the same jurisdiction.[17] Again, prison overcrowding presents critical problems for state governments. In an era of stringent budgetary constraints, moneys spent on the maintenance of huge prison establishments and their enlargements often represent funds taken from educational programs, welfare services, and infrastructure repairs. Yet the primary determinants of prison population are the decisions of local prosecutors and judges who bear no responsibility either for prison administration or for other state governmental programs affected by burgeoning prison populations.[18] There is no intelligible policy relating to the use of the death penalty even within states in which capital punishment is frequently employed. The caprice created by the unregulated discretion of individual prosecutors not only raises somber issues of inequity and discrimination but also confuses whatever purposes the death penalty may be thought to serve.[19] Fragmentation of discretionary authority, by blurring policy objectives and hampering law enforcement operations, must often obstruct American criminal justice from achieving its essential purposes. Such failures have a significance extending beyond matters of efficiency. The persistent inability of the system of criminal justice to achieve its critical overarching goals tends to encourage abuses of legal authority by those entrusted with operation of the system and to induce the public to tolerate erosion of the legality values.

Fragmentation of authority in the United States, however, is not peculiar to the administration of criminal justice but, rather, characterizes the operations of American political institutions more generally. The sundering of executive and legislative functions in our constitutional system; the distribution of lawmaking authority among legislatures, courts, administrative agencies, and political subdivisions; the continuing significance of divisions of sovereignty between federal and state governments; and the further distributions of authority among agencies and officers of state and local governments all testify to a political tradition suspicious of concentrations of official power. The principle of localism has from the beginning played a central role in American political attitudes. Thomas M. Cooley, writing in the nineteenth century, asserted that "the American system is one of complete decentralization, the primary and vital idea of which is, that local affairs shall be managed by local authorities . . . . The system is one which almost seems a part of the race to which we belong."[20] Nor has the ideal of decentralized political authority lost its appeal with the passage of time, as current political developments reveal.[21] That the fear of concentrated political authority in the administration of criminal justice is not frivolous is sufficiently demonstrated by the history of despotic regimes in the present century. Yet the rule-of-law values are not achieved simply through fragmentation of governmental authority. Indeed, as our own history makes clear, such decentralization of the American system of criminal justice often renders it unaccountable and thus erects formidable obstacles to the realization of the legality ideal.

We cannot repeal our history; the fragmentation of American criminal justice is in some part inherent in our constitutional system. But much that has evolved in the administration of criminal justice was by no means inevitable and with effort may be subject to modification. A great part of American practice in the criminal justice areas is to be explained less by political theory than by the influence of groups that perceive their self-interest to lie in maintaining a largely unsupervised functioning of independent local agencies. The problems of imposing accountability on officers and agencies engaged in administering criminal justice are of particular difficulty. A perception of the difficulties, however, should not obscure the many opportunities at hand for developing more robust habits of legality than now prevail. A brief consideration of the opportunities as well as the limitations that beset their realization seems now required.

II

The police function provides a prime instance of critical governmental activity in which discretionary decision making is endemic and, in the United States, one in which problems of establishing the locus of governing discretion are frequently unaddressed and unresolved.[22] The number of decisions officers, are required to make during the course of police patrol and the unpredictability of the problems they encounter preclude the possibility of a code of rules adequate to provide them detailed guidance in advance for many of the decisions they must make.

There are some police decisions, however, that from the beginnings of the modern era have been subject to legal rules administered by courts. Prominent among such norms are those seeking to limit the uses of force, especially deadly force, by persons executing arrests and performing other law enforcement obligations.[23] In recent years the devastating explosions of violence in urban ethnic communities, often ignited by police resort to firearms and other forms of extreme force, have resulted in the emergence of legal criteria more limiting and articulate than ever before. As the Supreme Court noted in 1985 when announcing new constitutional standards governing official uses of deadly force against persons fleeing felony arrest, many American police agencies had on their own initiatives already imposed restrictions on their members at least as rigorous as those found to be required by the Fourth Amendment.[24] The alacrity with which many police administrators moved to anticipate judicial action in this area is hardly surprising. Massive community disturbances create problems of public order that the police cannot contain.[25] The problems, however, go well beyond those of violence, fire, and looting while riots are in progress. They also involve difficulties in day-to-day patrol, for a perception in the communities of widespread improvident uses of extreme force by the police may inhibit the affected population from reporting the commission of crimes and identifying criminals, forms of community cooperation essential to effective performance of routine police functions.[26] The application of stringent rules to control uses of extreme force by police officers is thus seen as necessary to their self-interest and the functions they perform.

Yet the perceptions of police administrators are not necessarily those of some officers in the rank and file. New constitutional criteria and departmental regulations have not eliminated unjustified uses of deadly force by police officers on routine patrol. The instances are not confined to highly publicized cases, like those in Los Angeles and Detroit in the early 1990s.[27] A none-too-conscientious scrutiny of the press over a limited time interval will disclose continuing and numerous episodes of allegedly illegal police violence reported from all parts of the country.[28] Experience gained since the Watts riots in the 1960s strongly suggests that when police initiatives involving possibilities of death or serious physical injury are involved, the existing forms of guidance and oversight—those provided by courts and by departmental regulations—are insufficient to the task. Extension of external administrative controls involving greater participation by the larger community is required, for both the definition of appropriate police procedures and the discipline of officers transgressing the stipulated norms. Civilian administrative scrutiny and direction, not surprisingly, have traditionally been resisted by police organizations.[29] In part, the stance is that of any closely knit group responding to the threat of external interference. In some instances, however, opposition by the police is not merely reflexive or entirely unfounded. Police organizations have sometimes rightly feared intrusions of civilian authority as a means for introducing nefarious political influences into departmental operations, a fear that, unfortunately, is not always groundless.[30] Too much is at stake, however, to give such fears dispositive weight. All controls of public functions, whether imposed internally or externally, are accompanied with potentialities for inefficiency and corruption. Such possibilities define, in part, the difficulties surrounding a constructive social response to the problem of illegal police violence. An effective response is nevertheless urgent, for the present situation threatens the bonds of urban society.

For many persons not primarily concerned with criminal

justice administration and for some who are, the question of legal controls of police behavior is most easily seen as a matter of judicial interventions to preserve the constitutional rights of persons targeted by the system. Under the leadership of the Supreme Court, not only during the era of the Warren Court but before and after, a formidable and highly volatile body of constitutional doctrine pertaining to the rights of suspected persons has emerged, much of it associated with the application of exclusionary rules of evidence as devices to enforce the constitutional mandates. Although other nations have articulated judicial principles relating to police behavior and some have dealt with certain of the problems as those of constitutional law, in no other political society have the courts assumed such large responsibilities for the decency and efficacy of criminal justice as have the courts in the United States.[31] Identifying the reasons for the American judicial activism may prove instructive. A central explanation for the phenomenon must surely be that the courts, with varying degrees of awareness, have attempted to compensate for the failure of American institutions to fashion devices and practices effective to monitor and direct police activity, comparable to those achieved in other democratic societies.[32] It can hardly be asserted that judicial power by its nature is well adapted to the task of supervising systems of penal justice. Especially in regulating police behavior, judges operate under severe handicaps. The courts possess no plenary power to govern the day-to-day activities of police organizations. Judges speak only when some affected individual comes before the court and claims violation of his or her rights by official misconduct. Inevitably, many matters important to the decency and efficacy of criminal justice never arise in litigation, and other matters, only sporadically. As Chief Justice Earl Warren recognized, the effectiveness of the exclusionary rule is limited to a narrow area of police activity;[33] some have estimated the fraction at only 2% or 3%.[34] Moreover, the restiveness of the modern Court in administering the constitutional law of criminal procedure is more than evident: significant limitations have been imposed on the exclusionary rules, and substantive constitutional rights have been redefined and their scopes diminished.[35] It is of great importance that American courts maintain a vigorous stance in the areas of criminal justice, which is true not only because the rights of persons proceeded against require effective judicial protection but also because the courts are in a position to encourage the development within police organizations of administrative measures leading to more effective rule-of-law guidance of police discretion.[36] Yet all experience suggests that reliance primarily on judicial interventions to achieve adequate expression of the legality values in the administration of penal justice has and will continue to fail. What is required is institution building within the criminal justice systems, an insight perhaps not yet adequately reflected in much contemporary legal scholarship.[37]

The central rule-of-law issues emerging from the exercise of the police function in the United States are those of a radical paucity of law. Wide areas of police activity and decision making, some of great moment to the affected individuals, are governed by nothing that can be identified as a system of articulate norms. A great part of such unregulated exercises of power stems from the discretion of the police to determine when or whether criminal statutes will be enforced and what quantum of time and resources will be expended in enforcement efforts.[38] That such discretion, often unacknowledged, exists and is in some measure unavoidable is a conclusion reinforced by empirical observation of police operations. Police discretion to determine when and under what circumstances criminal statutes are to be enforced arises from a number of sources. Most important of these is the inescapable reality that no police organization, however zealous, possesses resources sufficient to give full enforcement to all criminal regulations. The incapacity of the organization to achieve full enforcement creates the necessity of rationing efforts and allocating resources. Decisions not to arrest or otherwise enforce criminal laws are made at all levels of the police hierarchy. Some of the decisions represent spontaneous and unconsidered judgments of individual officers on police patrol, and some constitute department-wide policies or practices. Thus the organization may find it necessary to determine whether drug enforcement is to be proactive, with substantial resources invested in ferreting out criminal offenses, or whether it is to be passive, with arrests being made only when violations come fortuitously to the officers' attention. Again, a police department in a university community may opt to neglect citywide enforcement for a time and concentrate its resources on detecting and apprehending a serial killer who has terrorized the college campus.[39]

Police discretion to determine when and how the criminal laws are to be enforced is not to be explained wholly, however, by reference to limitations of time, money, and personnel. Another source of such discretion is the nature of the criminal legislation the police are directed to enforce. Statutory criminal laws are often poorly drafted, obscure as to the conduct prohibited or the persons encompassed within its terms. One of the consequences of badly drafted laws is a transfer of what are essentially lawmaking functions from a legislature to the courts, prosecutors, and police, who are required to apply them. At times the delegation of lawmaking authority by the legislature to the enforcement agencies is deliberate, if unspoken: the legislators may intend that the enacted statute not be enforced at all or that it be applied only in special circumstances not stipulated in its provisions.[40] The legislature may believe that the language of the statute must be overbroad to ensure coverage of its intended targets, leaving it to the police and the prosecutors to withhold application to others falling within the statute's literal terms.[41]

The extraordinary range and variety of functions demanded of the police strongly affect the habits of legality displayed in American law enforcement. Much urban police activity consists of the performance of what are essentially welfare services, even though conducted through the powers and apparatus of criminal justice. The problems created by habitual drunkenness and alcoholic addiction impose major burdens on police operations. Because of the absence of alternative means, police officers are called on to employ powers of arrest, jail detention, and even criminal convictions for public drunkenness in their attempts to contain the situations presented.[42] Because such official activities are often motivated less by the usual objectives of criminal law enforcement than by such purposes as securing the physical survival of homeless alcoholic persons, police response is highly informal and assumes an almost unlimited dispensing authority. The assumption of power by the police to withhold applications of legal prohibitions in the interests of some conception of individualized need or individualized justice, however, is by no means confined to what have been described as welfare services. Throughout the broader range of their activities, the police are often sensitive to the harshness and apparent futility of arrests in particular cases and frequently elect not to invoke the criminal process. Nor would the community likely choose that they be wholly deprived of such dispensing authority. The late Judge Charles Breitel once remarked, "If every policeman . . . performed his responsibility in strict accordance with rules of law, precisely and narrowly laid down, the criminal law would be ordered but intolerable."[43] Thus, few would demand that a 17-year-old be arrested for a curfew violation when it is clear that her presence on the streets was caused by the breakdown of the bus on which she was riding. Yet however appealing the determination of the officer to abstain from arrest in the case supposed, we should not overlook the potential for arbitrary and unequal exercises of official power inherent in such unsupervised decision making. For on the same evening that the incident in question occurred, a second teenager in a similar situation may have been arrested by a different police officer and forced to spend the night in a juvenile detention center.[44]

The inevitability of discretionary decision making and the various factors that separate its exercise from effective legal controls tend to the formation of distinctive attitudes among the police toward the law and about their own central function. The overriding purpose of the police is seen to be that of preventing crime and disorder from reaching levels that produce alarm and outcry in the community. The criminal law tends to be viewed largely in instrumental terms, as a tool to be employed or disregarded depending on what contributions its application may be expected to make to the overriding objective.[45] Efforts to keep the lid on may result in significantly varying enforcement policies in different parts of the city. Police judgments of what kinds and levels of enforcement are consistent with the habits and desires of the inhabitants of a given urban community may be highly fallible and typically vary strongly among individual officers making such appraisals. A policy of leniency toward offenders committing aggravated assaults in the black ghetto while policies of strict enforcement are applied in white middle-class areas of the city may condemn residents of the former to conditions of violence deplored by many of its inarticulate inhabitants.[46]

The problems of containing and directing the dispensing powers of the police, it need hardly be said, are of great difficulty. At the outset, realistic efforts to regulate such discretion are obstructed by persistent refusals of police organizations to acknowledge that the discretion exists and is routinely exercised. In certain jurisdictions the posture is strengthened by statutes that purport to place on the police an obligation of "full enforcement" of all criminal laws.[47] Even in jurisdictions in which no such statutory mandates exist, the police are reluctant to concede the exercise of dispensing authority, for it opens the department to the pressures of those persons who deplore and also those who solicit such treatment. Even if the reality of police discretion to withhold application of the criminal law be fully acknowledged, special problems exist in identifying when and by whom it is exercised and in guiding its application. Many decisions by patrol officers to withhold arrests in cases of law violations remain undisclosed both to the public and to the higher echelons of the police department.[48]

Progress toward a fuller realization of legality values in police operations lies less in attempts to deny discretion to police personnel than in strategies for centralizing the locus of the governing discretion. Police decisions undertaken consistently with department-wide directives possess numerous advantages over decisions reflecting only the experience, judgment, and perhaps prejudices of individual officers. In many instances the precise content of departmental regulations may be less important than the existence of a considered departmental policy, for a uniform policy advances equal treatment of those persons subjected to penal authority and diminishes the influences of ethnic and religious prejudices, of the economic or social status of the persons proceeded against, and of pure caprice in police operations. The reports of individual officers to their superiors make possible the pooling of departmental experience and thereby contribute to the good sense and realism of departmental policy.[49] Articulate regulations extending over a broad range of problems important to both the police and the community may strengthen the position of the department when police action is challenged in court. The Supreme Court, when determining the constitutional validity of police action, has on occasion given weight to the fact that the police measures were taken pursuant to a previously articulated departmental policy rather than pursuant to the unguided discretion of an individual officer.[50] No doubt the courts are capable of doing considerably more than has been done to encourage internal rule making within police organizations.

Yet significant progress toward invigorating the habits of legality in American police operations requires more than the strengthening of internal rule making, with occasional and sporadic scrutiny by the courts when complaints of constitutional violation arise. External and jurisdiction-wide agencies that possess continuing authority to scrutinize the governance of local police operations and to create and enforce standards of policy and legality are required.[51] Steps toward that objective, if they occur, will no doubt be incremental. It is important that even small steps be taken.[52] A commentator in the 1980s identified the "apparent decision-channeling effect of prior training, professional incentives, managerial supervision on the job, and administrative and judicial review after the fact" as a leading characteristic of West German policing.[53] No one would likely apply a similar description to the performance of the police function in the United States. European models, of course, are in many respects inappropriate to American conditions. Those conditions include aspects of political structure and accompanying traditions and attitudes that limit a fuller realization of the legality values. Yet room for movement and reform exists. What is required is will and ingenuity.

A second major concentration of unregulated official discretion within the structure of American criminal justice is that of prosecutors. In 1941, Attorney General Robert Jackson stated, with little hyperbole, that "[t]he prosecutor has more control over life, liberty, and reputation than any other

person in America."[54] The impact of unsupervised prosecutorial decision making on the coherence of criminal
policy in the United States and the limitations it often imposes on realization of legality values were frequently
alluded to in the second chapter and require no large elab-
oration here.

The exercise of discretion by prosecutors is not peculiar
to American criminal justice but appears to be inherent in
the prosecutorial function wherever it is exercised.[55] Even
in nations that impose on prosecutors formal obligations to
bring to trial all cases in which adequate evidence of criminal guilt is available, a discretion to determine whether the
evidence is in fact adequate may remain largely with the
prosecutors; perhaps the conclusions reached sometimes
reflect other unacknowledged factors.[56] The exercise of
judgment on such issues as whom to charge, what levels
of punishment to seek, where the limited resources of the
prosecutor's office can best be concentrated is not only necessary but is salutary when wisely done and appropriately
regulated. What distinguishes American prosecutors is the
breadth of their unregulated discretionary authority. Even
in Great Britain, where attitudes toward the prosecutorial
function are nearer to those in the United States than to
those elsewhere in Europe,[57] Parliament has prescribed the
formulation of prosecution guidelines.[58]

Unregulated prosecutorial discretion in the United States
finds its origins, to considerable degree, in the traditions of
localism that characterize much of American political life. In
the states, the prosecutor is most often an elected official
with an independent power base. In many instances he will
be the most powerful political figure at the county level of
government and, as such, fully capable of eluding any minimal efforts at centralized supervision that may be attempted.
In the federal system the Department of Justice's regulation
of local prosecutorial decisions may be more meaningful,
but in many cases, including some of the most important
categories of federal crime, the Department has chosen to
afford only minimal guidance.[59] Suggestions for more active
centralized supervision of the prosecutorial function in
United States attorneys' offices can breed fierce and vocal
resistance.[60] The contrast of institutional organization of

prosecution in the United States with that in many continental countries and in Japan could hardly be more striking. In the latter, prosecution is ordinarily viewed as a lifetime career. It rarely serves as a stepping-stone to high political office, and members of the organization are protected from political interference and retaliation. Prosecutors share common backgrounds and training, develop primary allegiances to a national system of justice, and act within a structure of strong internal controls and administrative oversight.[61]

There are other sources of prosecutorial discretion in the United States. As in the case of the police, the breadth and imprecision of much criminal legislation confer on prosecutors important lawmaking powers. In some areas of legislation, like the federal Mail Fraud and Wire Fraud Acts, the present meanings ascribed to the statutes are largely the products of prosecutorial initiatives.[62] Recent years have seen significant expansions of prosecutorial discretion produced by a number of factors, among the most important being the weight of numbers oppressing the operations of American criminal justice. Backlog pressure in prosecutors' offices and in the courts encourage, if not dictate, dismissal of criminal charges capable of being proved in court or reduction of their severity through the processes of plea bargaining.[63]

It is not true, of course, that the power of the American prosecutor is wholly unconstrained. Community pressures, media publicity, and political influences may, on occasion, limit and direct prosecutorial action. These influences, however, may as often frustrate as advance rule-of-law values and sometimes represent precisely the sorts of interventions that prosecutors should be protected against.[64] The grand jury, when it is employed, may influence prosecutorial procedures but rarely provides genuine constraints on the exercise of discretion.[65] Prosecutors as officers of the courts in which they appear may be subject to a variety of judicial controls. The invalidity of prosecutorial action resulting in racial or religious discrimination has for many years been part of American public law.[66] In varying degrees throughout the country, judges participate in the processes of plea bargaining, and their influence is often important in determining when bargains will be attempted and what their terms may be. Yet the most generous estimates of judicial restraints on prosecutorial decision making reveal the influence to be small. The statement of Newman Baker in his pioneering studies of the American prosecutor more than 60 years ago describes a situation largely present today: "[T]he prosecutor is in practice substantially immune to judicial accountability for the noncorrupt exercise of his power not to initiate criminal prosecutions."[67]

The need for greater supervision and coordination of the prosecuting function in the United States is not a new perception. Written standards to guide the actions and decisions of staff members have been voluntarily adopted in some prosecutors' offices. The American Bar Association's *Standards Relating to the Administration of Criminal Justice* may have encouraged many such initiatives.[68] Internal guidelines in a single office, while useful, fall far short, however, of what is needed. Such measures afford no avenues for public participation in creating standards of acceptable practice in the performance of vital prosecutorial functions. They provide no external monitoring of how the functions are performed. Nor do they go far to mitigate the system-wide inconsistencies in present practice that often imperil equal treatment of those caught up in the criminal process and frequently frustrate achievement of coherent penal policy. More than a quarter century ago, the President's Commission on Law Enforcement and the Administration of Justice called for enhanced centralized supervision of prosecutorial activity in state jurisdictions.[69] If progress is to be made toward bringing much American prosecutorial practice within the boundaries of the rule of law, measures like those urged by the President's Commission will be required.

That broad areas of American criminal justice are characterized by a radical paucity of articulated norms for guiding the actions and decisions of public officers is a perception obvious to all who trouble to observe the system's operations. Efforts to reduce the pervasive normlessness in certain facets of the system have not been entirely absent. Of such efforts, none is more instructive in exposing the difficulties and dilemmas likely to be encountered in attempts at rule-of-law reform than those associated with the formulation and application of judicial sentencing guidelines, especially in the federal courts. The topic is of considerable technical complexity and one that in recent years has given rise to a formidable literature.[70] Only a few salient features of that ongoing experience can be noted here.

Few exercises of official authority produce greater impact on the lives of persons than does the judicial sentencing of convicted offenders. Discretionary sentencing has always given rise to concerns about possibilities of its arbitrary and inconsistent exercise. In the last third of the present century, however, unease engendered by the almost wholly unregulated applications of such powers became widespread, a development perhaps related to the decline of the rehabilitative ideal in correctional thought and practice and strengthened by the egalitarian thrust of social attitudes during and immediately following the Vietnam War. In 1973 the unease was given impressive statement by Marvin Frankel. "The sentencing powers of the judge," he wrote, "are, in short, so far unconfined that, except for frequently monstrous maximum limits, they are effectively subject to no law at all."[71]

One of the responses to the problems perceived in unregulated discretionary sentencing was the movement to establish guidelines to direct and constrain the exercise of judicial sentencing powers. The movement began in the states, notably in Minnesota.[72] Pursuant to the Sentencing Reform Act of 1984, the United States Sentencing Commission was established, and in 1987 the first federal sentencing guidelines and accompanying regulations became effective.[73] The Commission's work product has ever since prompted angry debate and protest.

Efforts to subject judicial sentencing to mandatory norms rest on the perception that unregulated discretion results in widespread sentencing disparities. The concept of disparity, however, is not self-defining. No two cases are identical in all respects, and whether differing sentences in similar cases constitute disparity depends on what factors are deemed relevant for purposes of comparison.[74] If two offenders, one of whom has had no prior convictions, receive equal prison terms for similar crimes of embezzlement, the sentences are disparate only if the absence of prior criminality is accepted as relevant to the determination of appropriate sentencing levels.[75] Yet the definitions of disparity are crucial in efforts to remedy arbitrariness in the sentencing process. Designating the factors that determine when penalties are to be enhanced or lessened implicates the deepest convictions concerning what a decent and efficacious system of criminal justice should be and guarantees discord and controversy when, as will most often be the case, such basic convictions are in conflict.

It was probably inevitable that any system of sentencing norms and procedures formulated in the 1980s would strongly reflect the contemporary popular and official attitudes toward widespread crime and its containment. Sentencing guidelines made their appearance in the federal courts at a time when the American "war on crime" was at or near its peak of intensity.[76] Two dominant characteristics of the war on crime are the demand for greater severity of criminal penalties and neglect of the requirements of penal proportion.[77] Both tendencies are abundantly expressed in the work product of the Sentencing Commission. The guidelines place new and enlarged reliance on prison incarceration to achieve the goals of criminal justice and have been an important contributing factor in the burgeoning of federal prison populations. The incidence of probation since the guidelines, the Commission observed in one of its annual reports, has been cut by more than half.[78] Nor has the Commission revealed significant interest or ingenuity in promoting intermediate penalties within the federal system, sanctions of a severity falling between probation, on the one hand, and imprisonment, on the other.[79] What has been most disturbing to many observers is the neglect of offender characteristics and situational factors in defining grounds for mitigating penalties.[80] An undue fixation on the crime and its resulting harm at the expense of traditional mitigating factors not only results in enhanced severity of criminal sanctions but also impedes the achievement of an equitable proportion between the culpability of offenders and the penalties imposed on them. Critics have pointed to a range of absurdities in the application of the guidelines[81] and have, with reason, deplored certain decisions of the Commission that tend to the expansion of unregulated discretion of prosecutors while reducing judicial sentencing options.[82]

Whatever differences may arise in formulating the critique, many informed observers would likely join in the judgment that current efforts to contain and direct the sentencing discretion of federal judges have to date proved less than successful. It would be erroneous, to conclude, however, that the difficulties encountered in the endeavor are solely the products of a particular stage of history, a period in which the thrust toward punitiveness overcomes all countervailing values. The most intractable problems may prove to be those inherent in efforts to contain and direct exercises of official power within the criminal justice system, whenever they may be undertaken. The basic difficulty involves the reconciliation of what are often conflicting values, each of which, however, has rule-of-law significance. The conflict is that between the search for individualized justice and the aspiration to subject the exercise of discretion to governing norms.[83] The problems created by imposing sentencing norms that inadequately incorporate factors important to achieving a reasonable proportion between culpability and penalty have been all too evident in recent experience. Such guidelines frequently engender a sense of injustice that leads to efforts to evade the guidelines through plea bargaining and otherwise, thereby shifting the locus of discretion from court to prosecutor and compromising the regulatory efficacy of official norms.[84]

An uninhibited pursuit of individualized justice, however, produces outcomes equally unacceptable. The quest for sentences perfectly commensurate with culpability may incur substantial social costs. Limits imposed on the consideration of such mitigating factors as the economic, cultural, moral, or intellectual deprivations sustained by offenders in the past may amount to a healthy recognition of the limited capacities of juries and judges to identify and evaluate such factors.[85] A certain conservatism in defining the scope of mitigating authority may sometimes, therefore, reflect more than considerations of bureaucratic convenience. It may, in addition, rest on an awareness that the exercise of open-ended mitigating authority is peculiarly vulnerable to inconsistency and caprice in the sentencing process.

It is apparent that what is most required are good-faith efforts to balance the aspirations of government by rule and those of individualized justice so that, in some measure, both may be reflected in the sentences imposed. Achieving an accommodation of the sometimes conflicting goals cannot be easy, and the effort may appear uninspiring. The alternative, however, is an angry polarization of views that may cause us to forget or underestimate the considerations that originally prompted sentencing reform. Administration of guidelines in some state systems of justice provides grounds for belief that a feasible balancing of values in criminal sentencing is attainable.[86]

III

The radical paucity of legal norms, widespread and pervasive as it is, is only one of the circumstances in American criminal justice contributing to the weakness of institutional habits of legality. Ironically, other significant obstacles to the realization of legality values have their origins in the principal lawmaking agencies of society, the courts, and legislatures.

It is of more than historical interest that in the eighteenth-century literature on which much of the modern ideal of legality rests, the primary threats to a regime of law are seen to emerge less from exertions of executive and legislative power than from the conduct of magistrates. Beccaria in his famous essay identifies usurpation by judges of their proper roles as the first of the ills necessary to be overcome if criminal justice founded on the rule of law is to be achieved. "The disorders that may arise from a rigorous observance of the letter of penal laws," he wrote, "are not to be compared with those produced by the interpretation of them."[87]

The interpretative function of appellate courts in the United States is crucial to rule-of-law concerns in criminal cases. Much of the substantive content of American criminal law is a product of appellate court determination, and, given the prevailing tendencies of legislative lawmaking, the judicial contribution appears to be increasing. It may be freely conceded that retroactive lawmaking by the courts in the course of interpreting and applying statutes is in some measure inescapable. Ambiguity in statutory law stems from more than legislative ineptness in framing statutory language. Legislative texts of any generality regularly give rise to questions of meaning and application in situations that were not and could not have been anticipated in the legislative process. The resolution of such questions can only be accomplished in the courts.[88] Yet it is equally apparent that the methods and style of statutory interpretation characteristic of other legal systems are significantly different from our own. Even in the interpretation of criminal statutes, American judges tend to readings less restricted by the ordinary meanings of the language employed in the official texts.[89] Excursions into "legislative history," prohibited or rarely undertaken elsewhere, are among the conspicuous features of American judicial practice, even when, as is frequently true, the meanings to be derived from the materials of legislative history are considerably less determinate than the meanings capable of being gained from the language of the statute.[90] Although principles of statutory interpretation are often discussed in American judicial opinions and in the critical literature, there appears to be little consensus on what the governing principles are, what priorities are to be assigned to them, or what their meanings are in actual application. In short, both the theory and practices of statutory interpretation reveal an incoherence and fragmentation that perhaps echo those typical of American political institutions generally. It is part of academic "street wisdom" to attribute the comparatively unconstrained practices of many American judges to some inherent indeterminacy of language and an inescapable ambiguity of legal rules. It should be noted, however, that British judges, employing a somewhat similar English language, produce a style of interpretation both different from and more restrained than our own.[91] It appears much closer to truth to say that the practices and habits revealed by American judges when confronting criminal statutes are products of a legal culture strongly conditioned by the latitudes inevitable in constitutional adjudication and by the unique relationship of courts and legislatures in the American system.

The importance of an interpretive style that gives predominant weight to the ordinary meanings of statutory language is particularly urgent in judicial readings of penal legislation. Interpretations departing from ordinary meanings and founded on notions of ultimate legislative purpose may often conflict with basic *nulla poena* values. Communication to the citizenry of what behavior runs the peril of sanctions should, to the extent possible, be effective from the date of the statute's enactment.[92] I am reminded of the statement offered in Saul Bellow's novel *Mr. Sammler's Planet:* "All mapmakers should place the Mississippi in the same location, and avoid originality. It may be boring, but one has to know where he is . . . ."[93] Interpretations grounded on ordinary meanings and on purposes reasonably inferable from the language of statutes are likely to come closer to the elusive "intent" of the legislature as a whole. Most voting members do not participate in the committee processes before enactment of any particular bill, and their understandings, like those of the individual citizen, are likely to be based on the ordinary meanings of the language employed in the text.[94] Once an interpretation of an ambiguous statutory provision is made in the appellate courts, it should ordinarily be adhered to in subsequent cases. Deviations in judicial interpretation compound the ills of uncertainty first introduced into the statute at the legislative level.[95]

The mild strictures just stated are frequently ignored in the functioning of state and federal courts. Notions of "strict" interpretation of penal statutes appear to have insecure footing in the practices of most American judges.[96] The principle seems rarely to determine outcome and, when mentioned at all, serves chiefly to articulate results reached largely on other grounds. In the Racketeer Influenced and Corrupt Organizations (RICO) legislation, Congress directed that "the provisions of this title shall be liberally construed to effectuate its remedial purposes," an invitation that most federal judges appear to have accepted with some alacrity.[97] The modern "meanings" of the federal Mail Fraud Act result from prosecutorial initiatives and judicial lawmaking having only the most tenuous connections with the language of

the statute.[98] If the Supreme Court can rule, as it recently
has, that a provision enhancing penalties for a crime in
which a gun is "used" can be read to cover a case in which
the gun was not employed as a weapon but, rather, was
given in payment for illegal drugs,[99] then the federal courts'
commitments to the strict interpretations of penal directives
and the courts' inclinations to be guided by the ordinary
usages of language in the contexts presented must be
doubted.

The tendency of American judges to approach the tasks
of statutory interpretation and other nonconstitutional adjudication with much the same latitude as may be appropriate
for construing such protean constitutional mandates as "due
process of law" and "equal protection of the laws" has
evoked surprise from some foreign observers of our judicial
institutions.[100] The habits acquired by judges in constitutional litigation, reinforced by the dominating influences of
public-law instruction and scholarship in the law schools,
may well have importantly affected American styles of statutory interpretation.[101] Less speculative and at least equally
significant, however, are the nature of the legislative process
in the United States and the consequent relationships that
connect performance of the judicial and legislative functions.

The absence of a consistent and coherent interpretative
methodology in the appellate courts reflects the lack of coherence in the processes of legislative lawmaking. A large
part of criminal legislation, including that produced by Congress, is not "good" law, if the term is used, not to describe
the substantive policies expressed in the statutes, but rather
is used as a measure of the statutes' clarity, coherence, and
contributions to citizen self-guidance. The texts of American
legislation are rarely subjected to a scrutiny and discipline
comparable to those supplied by the Office of Parliamentary
Counsel in Great Britain. There, principles and conventions
of statutory expression have evolved over the years and are
applied consistently by a staff of civil servants whose efforts
are concentrated on the drafting function.[102] The conventions employed in the drafting are generally well understood
by the judiciary, and hence questions of legislative purpose
and meanings are significantly reduced.[103] Amendments of

legislative proposals from the floor, a major source of technical insufficiency in American legislation, are subjected to exercises of executive authority in parliamentary systems that drastically limit the legislative initiatives of individual members.[104] The fragmentation and diffusion of authority of American legislative bodies have been defended as promoting a greater responsiveness to public demands than may be typical of other political systems. Such benefits may be thought to outweigh the losses sustained through the technical deficiencies of the legislative product. There are practices of American legislatures, however, difficult to justify by any theory of public benefit. One of these is the growing tendency of Congress to enact voluminous omnibus crime bills containing remarkable varieties of crime definitions, penalties, and procedures.[105] The very bulk of the legislation reduces the likelihood that its provisions will receive genuine consideration by individual legislators and creates formidable obstacles to the effective scrutiny of proposals under consideration by the press and interested members of the public. The complexity of the omnibus bills has often led to omissions, inconsistencies, and confusion in the enacted laws.[106]

American courts confronted by obligations of interpreting and applying criminal statutes are not only required to resolve the inevitable ambiguities arising from efforts to order the future through legislation, but also often are faced with the remedial task of reformulating the provisions of inadequately articulated laws. How far the remedial function is to be pursued by American courts raises important issues involving the principle of democratic lawmaking by elected officials, as well as basic *nulla poena* concerns. The American legal culture encourages judges, in a degree unmatched in other legal systems, to conceive of themselves as partners of legislatures in governing the state or country. The judicial function is seen to include the task of furthering the ongoing governmental process.[107] Accordingly, deficient legislative products are to be refashioned in the courts when such judicial lawmaking is perceived as contributing to the more effective operation of the political institutions.

The concept of partnership between courts and legislatures, with the attendant implications of judicial activism,[108] must in considerable part reflect felt needs in the American system. Substantial modifications of the judicial role at this stage of history can hardly be anticipated. Yet present institutional practices incur substantial costs. The judicial role as currently defined and exercised in the United States contributes to legislative irresponsibility and obstructs initiatives for reform within legislative bodies. More than a century ago, James B. Thayer noted that the American doctrine of judicial review breeds an unhealthy reliance of legislatures on the courts and diminishes legislative concerns with the substance of constitutional rights.[109] In nonconstitutional areas, similar dependencies are revealed in legislative practice and with similarly unfortunate consequences. The alacrity with which courts come to the rescue of ailing legislation must often stifle efforts in the legislatures to produce more carefully articulated products. What is perhaps more serious is that the activist judicial stance permits legislatures to evade their obligations to determine substantive policy. The sometimes unconsidered reliance of legislators on the courts to resolve substantive issues posed by legislation may be illustrated by the following incident: A member of a state legislature who had just succeeded in getting a criminal statute enacted was asked the meaning of a particular provision. His answer was, "We don't know. The courts haven't spoken yet."

The quality of legislative performance in the framing of criminal statutes might be improved if the courts were to make clear the interpretive principles they propose to apply, particularly in areas in which chronic problems of meaning have arisen. One such area is illustrated by an English law, wholly typical of dozens of American statutes enacted each year. The English provision criminalizes one who "wilfully kills . . . a house dove."[110] The language contains a syntactical ambiguity, for it does not make clear whether the accused's liability depends on his knowing at the time of killing that the bird *was* a house dove. The ambiguity is important, for how it is resolved determines whether the statute imposes strict criminal liability or whether the prosecution is required to establish that the accused possessed a culpable mens rea.[111] Removal of the confusion presents a drafting problem of no difficulty, and the Model Penal Code provides useful illustrations of how such clarity may be achieved in the general provisions of the criminal code.[112] When the legislatures have not acted, the courts might well announce, consistently with the traditions of strict interpretation of penal laws, that full mens rea requirements will be assumed in all cases in which the matter has been left in doubt by the statute. The result may be a saving of judicial effort while supplying inducements to legislators to assume more fully their responsibilities for clear policy decisions.

Recent trends in criminal legislation enacted at the state, but particularly at the federal, level give rise to concerns about the erosion of legality values in American criminal law. The legislation is of concern both because of the vagueness of its basic definitions of the behaviors that are criminal and because of the consequent enlargement of powers of retroactive lawmaking by prosecutors and courts. The nature of the trends can perhaps be best understood by first noting a body of foreign legislation in which the tendencies have been realized in their most extreme and virulent forms.

The "security legislation" of the Republic of South Africa contains a body of enactments remarkable not only for their assaults on basic human rights of political participation and personal security but also for their systematic rejection of the formal requisites of the rule of law.[113] Although many of the provisions have been superseded, the legislation provides a vivid catalog of techniques employed by a repressive government and deserves continuing attention for many of the same reasons that still inspire the study of the Nazi dictatorship and other fallen totalitarian regimes. Perhaps the most striking attribute discerned on first approaching the South African legislation is the remarkable range of human activity it encompasses. Few, if any, significant areas of human behavior—social, political, or even personal—are immune from the threat of penal and administrative sanctions. Under the South African security laws, the notion of who is the criminal has few identifiable limits. Thus, a member of a crowd may be subject to draconian penalties when other persons, never identified, engage in acts of violence.[114] A person joining a school boycott because of the low level of services afforded the affected population may be found guilty of sabotage.[115] Anyone spreading a rumor "calculated" to "embarrass the government in the conduct of its foreign relations" is or may be a criminal.[116] The offender under this legislation is perhaps not Everyman, but the concept of criminality is extraordinarily inclusive.

Inevitably, expanding the concept of criminal behavior to include almost unlimited varieties of acts and omissions results in statutory definitions of crime that are vague and evanescent. The South African statutes are remarkable for the generality of the language employed. As recently as 1982, the Parliament provided penalties of 10 years' imprisonment for persons who advocate "any of the objects of communism."[117] The definition of "communism" provided by the statute does little to relieve the obscurity of the penal provision and indeed may add imponderables of its own.[118] Again, the enactment authorizes severe penalties for an offense called terrorism if the actor commits an act of violence with intent to "achieve, bring about or promote any constitutional, political, industrial, social or economic aim or change in the Republic."[119] Does the throwing of a stone through the company's window during a labor dispute trigger the statute?

Related to the pervasive vagueness of statutory articulation in these laws is the attribute of overbreadth. Even the punitive motivations of an authoritarian regime cannot ensure that all persons committing "acts of violence," however trivial, will be prosecuted and subjected to penalties for treason, as provided in the statute just mentioned. It may be impossible to prosecute and incarcerate all participants in a strike who may be said to have intended to "interrupt . . . the distribution . . . of petroleum products."[120] The breadth and inarticulateness of the provisions create a broad penumbra of doubt about the meanings of the law and to whom it may be made to apply. The uncertainties so engendered must, as intended, create devastating chilling effects on ordinary political expression and activity. Moreover, the vagueness and overbreadth result in delegation to police officials and the minister of justice of practical retroactive authority to determine the laws' meanings and applications. The discretion so delegated is largely unencumbered by norms and limitations enforceable in the courts. Indeed, the freeing of police and executive personnel from rule-of-law constraints was a calculated purpose of much South African legislation.

The distinguishing characteristics of the South African security laws, then, may be said to be those of remarkable breadth of attempted penal regulation, vagueness, over-breadth, and delegation of virtually unfettered authority to police and executive personnel. Can legitimate comparisons be drawn between these laws and some of the criminal statutes being administered in the federal courts today? It seems unmistakable that the current law of criminal conspiracy, the RICO legislation, and the latter-day versions of the Mail Fraud Act, to name a select few, do in some measure manifest characteristics clearly discernible in the South African legislation. It is equally true, of course, that the federal statutes' departures from the legality ideal are significantly less fundamental and virulent. The federal legislation, in general, does not directly assault basic rights of political participation, although recent applications of RICO appear to be generating First Amendment issues with increasing frequency.[121] The purposes of the federal legislation, unlike those of the South African laws, do not include the shoring up of a minority political regime. The federal laws are not flanked by a comparable array of administrative measures banning social contacts of individuals, banning organizations, authorizing broad and loosely regulated preventive detention, and shrouding prison administration in impenetrable secrecy. Yet it would be unjustifiably complacent to ignore the fact that federal criminal law increasingly reflects many of the departures from the legality ideal more clearly displayed in the South African security legislation. The tendency is and ought to be disconcerting to those who believe with Aristotle that the rule of law depends ultimately on the cultivation of the habits of legality in the routines of public life.

The dangers and deficiencies of the criminal-conspiracy concept as it has evolved in Anglo-American law have been stated so frequently that only brief comment is required here.[122] The gravest assaults on the rule of law by the conspiracy device may be grouped under two broad headings. First, the principles underlying conspiracy prosecutions are of such generality and imprecision as to afford inadequate direction to officials—prosecutors, judges, juries—who wield the public force. In consequence, numerous convictions are based, in fact, not on intelligible principles of preexisting law, but rather on law fashioned at the point of application to fit the contours of the particular case. The evidence marshaled by appellate courts when affirming conspiracy convictions not infrequently appears to be at least equally amenable to outcomes squarely contrary to those reached at trial and on appeal.[123] Second, the procedures and practices employed in adjudicating guilt in conspiracy trials, especially those involving multiple charges, numerous defendants, and issues of extreme complexity, are often incapable of satisfying standards of fairness and accuracy.[124] Substantive doctrines may fail of essential attributes of legality simply because they impose burdens on the adjudicatory process that it cannot sustain. In responding to the demands of adjudication, courts have formulated procedures, including those relating to the admissibility of evidence, that enlarge the dangers of mistakes and inequity.[125] The questions submitted to juries in large and complex conspiracy prosecutions, especially those pertaining to persons alleged to have acted on the fringes of a conspiratorial agreement, often cannot be resolved with reasonable prospects of justice to many of those placed in jeopardy of severe criminal sanctions.[126]

As recently as a generation ago, criticisms of conspiracy law and practices had reached a level of intensity to afford some optimism that progress toward a law of group crime more congruent with the legality ideal might, in the course of time, be achieved. In the intervening years, the war on crime, especially in drug law enforcement,[127] and the applications made of the conspiracy section of the RICO statute[128] have smothered these hopes and have, in fact, enlarged and exacerbated the uses and abuses of conspiracy prosecutions.

The federal RICO legislation[129] and the Mail Fraud and Wire Fraud Acts,[130] as reconstituted by the federal courts, have ambitious purposes. They are intended, among much else, to strike devastating blows on organized crime[131] and to punish public officials, state and federal, who betray their public trusts.[132] The scope of the ambitions influences the fundamental nature of the legislation. There is no focus on limited and readily identifiable segments of human behavior. Organized crime, however the term is understood, encompasses an extensive range of activity. Political corruption likewise exhibits a wide gamut of conduct. There is nothing here comparable to the comforting concreteness of a body sprawled on the floor in a homicide prosecution. These statutes, along with those relating to criminal conspiracy and a number of other federal offenses, occupy not the whole range of human activity but a very broad ambit, indeed.

The Mail Fraud Act has already been mentioned. The legislation, enacted in 1872 and amended in 1909, appears to have been directed to frauds resulting in pecuniary and property losses to the victims.[133] As such, it provided substantially wider applications than afforded by common-law principles.[134] In recent years, however, a remarkable expansion of the statute's range occurred in the federal courts of appeal. The limitations of traditional fraud law were ignored, and a doctrine of "intangible rights" evolved, the violation of which was equated with the statutory "scheme or artifice to defraud."[135] Thus a public official who accepts a bribe may be seen as defrauding the public of its rights to the faithful performance of official duties, even when no pecuniary loss to the public can be traced. The development of largely undefined concepts of fiduciary obligation resulted in imposing felony penalties on a practicing lawyer who, although guilty of a serious conflict of interests, seems not to have inflicted tangible loss on anyone.[136] A party official involved in a kickback scheme was convicted, leaving the line between legitimate and illicit political activity obscure and undefined.[137] When attempting a general description of the concept underlying the "intangible rights" cases, a lower court could achieve no greater precision than that it concerned "moral uprightness, fundamental honesty, fair play, and right dealing."[138]

The unease engendered by the obscurity of the concepts derived from the Mail Fraud and Wire Fraud Acts is enlarged by the problems of overbreadth they present. The problems may be illustrated by the applications of modern mail fraud law to cases of corrupt behavior by state and federal officials. Even if it were assumed that no serious difficulties exist in determining when officials violate the "intangible rights of the public," there remains the question of *which* of the almost innumerable instances of political corruption are to be prosecuted in the federal courts. That political motivations have at times powerfully influenced the selection of such cases for prosecution can hardly be doubted.[139] It is of more than trivial concern that granting United States attorneys a kind of roving commission to purify our public life may give rise to suspicions of improper motivation, even when the suspicions are not well founded.

It is generally understood that the dominant purpose of the RICO statute, when enacted, was to prevent or obstruct the infiltration of organized crime into legitimate business enterprises. It is also clear that the legislation has rarely been employed to achieve this end.[140] The statute defines four RICO offenses, each of which requires proof of a "pattern of racketeering activities."[141] To establish a "pattern", the prosecution must prove commission of at least two "predicate" offenses within a specified time.[142] These offenses are to be drawn from a list of some 10 broad categories of state crimes and almost 50 sections of the United States Code.[143] State legislation inspired by the RICO statute may embrace even broader varieties of criminal activity.[144] The RICO statute is not directed to a unitary concept of criminal behavior. Instead, it embraces a remarkable range of serious delinquent conduct.

It seems a fair generalization that whenever criminal legislation seeks to penalize such unusually broad swaths of behavior, language becomes general; and the lack of specificity often gives rise to issues of meaning. A series of such questions characterizes the history of RICO. One example is provided by *H.J., Inc. v. Northwestern Bell Telephone Co.,* a 1989 civil RICO case in the Supreme Court.[145] The question involved the meaning of the phrase "pattern of racketeering activities." The statute clearly requires proof of two predicate offenses within a specified time. But is this enough? Suppose the two predicate crimes are wholly unrelated. To have a "pattern," must there be "something more"? The Court concluded that something more is required, that proof of two predicate offenses only establishes the "outer limits" of the concept, albeit one "that is broad indeed."[146] Justice

William Brennan noted that the statute "conspicuously fails anywhere to identify . . . forms of relationship or external principles to be used in determining whether racketeering activity falls into a pattern for purposes of the Act."[147] The statute's deficiencies, naturally enough, had created widely differing readings among the courts of appeal.[148] In *Northwestern* the Court provides a formula in which elements of "relationship" and "continuity" are emphasized. That the formula does not approach full definition is freely conceded. "The development of these concepts," Justice Brennan wrote, "must await future cases, absent a decision by Congress to revisit RICO to provide clearer guidance to the Act's intended scope."[149]

It is instructive to reflect on what has occurred. A central provision of the RICO statute was inadequately defined. After almost two decades during which hundreds of RICO cases were prosecuted and in which sharp differences concerning the term's meaning were expressed in lower federal courts, the Supreme Court articulated a formula. The formula admittedly leaves open serious questions of application to future litigation. Such was the situation as the RICO statute entered the third decade of its history.

Other serious issues of meaning in basic provisions of the RICO statute have arisen. Even when the aggregation of large varieties of criminal activity within a single statutory definition does not pose serious problems of vagueness, it may result in criminal sanctions being applied in sensitive areas clearly not anticipated by the legislature and thus without the advantage of prior legislative deliberation. The possible applications of the RICO statute to the activities of antiabortion demonstrators provide one such example.[150]

The interpretative role of the federal courts when dealing with much modern criminal legislation is anything but easy. The frequent ineptness of statutory language, the scope of the provisions, and the ambiguities of legislative purpose have created difficulties for the courts that are substantial and time consuming. Criticisms of the judicial product must be tempered by awareness of the problems presented. Yet, granting the dimensions of the task with which the courts are confronted, certain tendencies of the judicial performance in recent years breed unease. What may be

most striking about the judicial reactions to the statutes under consideration are the breadth of the courts' readings of
statutory language and an eagerness, sometimes approaching avidity, of many federal judges to ratify prosecutors' initiatives and interpretations of federal criminal laws. In some
few instances reservations have been expressed and warn-
ings issued from the bench, but the current has not been
significantly diminished.[151] Missing in the interpretive style
is what might be called a proper judicial partisanship in
support of the legality ideal. When confronted by alternative
readings of ambiguous statutory provisions, the courts have
frequently selected those that most exacerbate rather than
reduce uncertainties in application of the statutes' terms,
thereby weakening the community's understanding of the
laws' commands and enhancing the unguided discretion of
public officials.[152]

Ultimately, however, the principal source of the problems just addressed lies less in the performance of courts
than in that of legislatures. It comes as no surprise to discover that the same impetus toward decentralization of authority and fragmentation of function observable in most
American institutions of criminal justice characterizes the
internal operations of American legislatures.[153] Nearly 80
years ago, Ernst Freund observed that "[t]he striking difference between legislation abroad and in this country is that
under every system except the American the executive government has a protected monopoly of legislative initia-
tive."[154] The weakness of centralized control of the lawmaking process contributes strongly to technical deficiencies in
the legislative product. More than this, however, it renders
less attainable a consistent *course* of legislative lawmaking
and, as has been noted, institutionalizes legislative dependency on the courts for performance of basic legislative
obligations.

It is clear that much in the functioning of American legislatures is genetically related to the broader political culture.
Radical transformation of the legislatures to conform to parliamentary models is not a realistic object of reform in the
United States, nor is it clear that such transformation, if attainable, would on balance serve the best interests of American society. Yet not all troublesome aspects of American leg-

islative practice are inherent in the system, and a greater
focusing of legal scholarship on ameliorating them might
well contribute to practical solutions.

The first and most fundamental issue of legislative policy
(and one that law school scholarship has often neglected)
concerns identification of those areas of behavior that are
appropriate for the introduction of criminal sanctions and
those that are not. It has been observed that many of the
modern tasks assigned to the criminal law give rise to serious issues of legality. In a leading case, the Court of Appeals for the Second Circuit remarks that the section of the
federal penal code describing the crime of mail fraud "is
seemingly limitless on its face."[155] The statement illumi-
nates a leading characteristic of much modern criminal legislation: its failure adequately to distinguish criminal from
noncriminal behavior. The purpose of crime definition is not
simply to facilitate the unleashing of governmental powers
against persons and groups but also, at the same time, to
make evident the behaviors that are immune from the oner-
ous intrusions of the state. It is this central and elementary
definitional obligation that is increasingly neglected in the
lawmaking of American legislatures and courts. If penal
regulation cannot be achieved without impairing the basic
decencies of the criminal justice process, if adequate warn-
ings cannot be given to potential offenders, and if adequate
guidance cannot be given to public officers empowered to
apply the law's provisions, then there are surely powerful
reasons to withdraw or withhold criminal penalties and to
seek noncriminal sanctions to achieve the goals of public
policy in the areas under consideration.[156] The modern arsenal of noncriminal sanctions is a formidable one, and
doubts about their effectiveness should not be permitted to
prevail until thorough consideration of alternative measures
is given.

Resort to criminal sanctioning is unlikely to become so
parsimonious, however, as totally to exclude invocations of
the criminal law in situations presenting significant threats
to legality values. One of the important movements in congressional lawmaking in this century, however debilitating
to the legislative functions, has been the enactment of open-
ended statutes, the precise regulatory content of which is

formulated, not by Congress, but by administrative officers and agencies.[157] One familiar example is the Occupational Safety and Health Act of 1970.[158] The primary congressional purpose of the Act, as stated in section 2(b), is "to assure so far as possible every working man and woman in the Nation safe and healthful working conditions to preserve our human resources."[159] The statute does not grapple with such pertinent questions as when working conditions are "safe" and "healthful" or what levels of expenditures and effort to achieve safety goals are to be demanded of employers. Instead, section 6 delegates the formulation of such directives to the administrative process.[160] It is doubtful that the standard of "dishonest behavior" that evolved in mail fraud litigation, for example, is significantly more amorphous than that of "safe and healthful working conditions" in the OSHA statute. There are profound differences, however, in the two kinds of regulation. The Occupational Safety and Health Act presupposes an administrative process that will produce and publish substantive regulations to direct the behavior of both employers and public officials. The Mail Fraud Act delegates no such obligations to any similar agency. The meanings of such concepts as "fundamental honesty" and "intangible rights of the public" are not defined by regulations before prosecution but instead emerge retroactively in the course of appellate review. If our public policy is increasingly to incorporate sweeping criminal regulation of highly variegated behavior, consideration might well be given to measures approaching the administrative model. The delegation of lawmaking powers by legislatures would at least possess the virtue of being overt and open to public view, and the resulting regulations could avoid much of the retroactive character inescapable in prosecutorial and judicial initiatives. Criminal prosecutions based on regulations would, of course, proceed in the courts, and their validity would be open to judicial review. Experience gained in the administrative process might in the course of time reveal possibilities for greater precision in the language of the regulations and offer greater flexibility in adapting the penal measures to the differing regulatory problems revealed.

There are other possibilities calling for exploration. One critical need in the operations of both state and federal legislative bodies is an internal mechanism that better audits the performance of already enacted legislation, that informs the legislative body of readings being given existing laws in the courts, and that identifies malfunctions in the administration of existing laws, difficulties that were not and some that could not have been anticipated at the time of enactment. The need for such mechanisms are particularly acute in the consideration of criminal legislation.[161] In some areas, such as taxation and economic regulation, contending and well-financed private interests and an alert and aggressive bar may assist in bringing such issues and information to the attention of legislative committees. No such process operates in committee consideration of most criminal legislation, and institutional devices are required to facilitate a rational course of lawmaking.

Although the objectives of reform of the legislative process cannot realistically encompass changes in the fundamental character of American legislatures, measures to improve the quality of legislation and those that may move legislative bodies toward fuller performance of their delegated responsibilities seem well within the realm of possibility. Efforts to achieve these ends have not been wholly neglected in American law schools. They are entitled, however, to higher priority.

4

Summation

The preceding discussion, encompassing a wide variety of contemporary and historical experience, rests on a series of underlying propositions. It proceeds, first, on the assumption that the rule-of-law concept is vital to the life and survival of liberal societies. Conceptual analysis, although essential to identification and resolution of critical issues, is insufficient to an understanding of the meanings and dimensions of the legality ideal in a functioning political society. To grasp the operational significance of the concept, we must look to the habitual behavior of public officials wielding the public force and to the levels of fidelity to law displayed in the community. It has also been asserted that the habits of legality practiced in the administration of criminal justice may be significantly weakened in times like the present and recent past, when fear and outrage are engendered by perceptions of rampant criminality. The resulting encroachments on the rights of individuals and disregard of the forms of law will likely not be confined to those situations in which emergencies are thought to arise but instead will extend to the operation of the system as a whole.

It has been argued in these comments, however, that the low vitality of the legality ideal in broad areas of American criminal justice is not alone a product of a passing time of troubles. It is to be explained in large measure by a decentralized and fragmented institutional structure—and per-

haps of equal importance, by attitudes and assumptions reinforced by the structure—that reduces the potency of legal
norms as a regulator of official behavior and leaves public
officers often substantially unaccountable for their uses of
public authority. These institutional characteristics resist
modification in part because they reflect aspects common
to American political institutions generally. Moreover, the
habits of legality struggle against the social and political
fragmentation of a pluralistic society. From the beginning,
American society has been notable for its competing attitudes determined by regional interests and by commitments
to groups defined by religious affiliation and belief, ethnic
antecedents, gender, and economic and ideological objectives. American pluralism has sometimes been praised, perhaps with reason, as a bulwark of individual freedom in
these times. Yet, ironically, pluralistic politics may impose
compromises of principle that erode habits of legality and, in
the long run, weaken the rule of law. One of the expressions
of American pluralism is the practice of single-issue politics
by groups of persons who are dedicated to the achievement
or prevention of certain results in limited areas of concern
and who manifest small interest in other objectives and aspirations. Such groups are strongly result oriented. They are
ordinarily not well informed about the fundamentals of the
legal system and are typically impatient with inhibitions of
any kind that may limit or obstruct their access to the public
force.[1]

The array of forces and factors weakening the vitality of
the rule of law in American criminal justice is surely formidable. Efforts to invigorate the habits of legality in these
areas are not an undertaking for the purist or the faint of
heart. It is a mark of maturity to recognize that political and
social objectives are rarely fully realized and that gains
achieved may be quickly lost for want of persistent and often
unrewarding labor. Yet the very difficulties encountered in
giving fuller expression to the legality ideal may provide the
best evidence of its importance.

Efforts to vitalize the legality ideal in institutional practices are obstructed by certain assumptions about the law
and its processes, entertained both in the universities and,
to some degree, in the wider community. As noted earlier,

nihilistic trends of thought in the form of a radical language skepticism and rule skepticism challenge not only the attainability of the rule of law but also the possibilities of law itself. Such expressions, although much discussed and widely purveyed, enlist only a limited constituency and do not constitute the most serious obstacles to responsible confrontation of legality issues. More significant are the attitudes of those persons who are unwilling to abandon wholly the traditions of legality but whose defense of the rule of law is conditioned by fears that its applications may often obstruct achievement of goals of social or individualized justice. That the virtue of legality is only one of the values important to a good society may be freely granted. The substantive content of its laws must serve basic human requirements. It is possible to conceive of a democratic legal society that observes all the *nulla poena* virtues of certainty, predictability, and consistency in its laws but that nevertheless enforces governmental policy fundamentally objectionable. As noted in the preceding discussions, tension created by the sometimes conflicting aspirations of government by rule and those of individualized justice can be clearly identified throughout the criminal justice process. In some few instances it may be the part of wisdom to permit strong equities in particular cases to prevail over the rule. Such accommodations, however, should be the product of conscious choice and be made with awareness of the dangers of unregulated arbitrary discretion.

There appears to be a widespread assumption in academic circles, not always fully articulated, that a basic disharmony exists between the substance and the forms of law and that the forms of law, however indispensable, obstruct the attainment of good laws. A central purpose of these remarks is to question the assumption and to suggest that the opposite is most often true: serious attention to the forms of law makes the achievement of substantively good law more likely. We may begin by noting what has been called the normative values of legality. The achievement of relative certainty and consistency in the law and its applications contributes importantly to the development of personal autonomy and a vital selfhood, substantive values of no small importance. The point, however, is a larger one. It is that the rule of law most often contributes to the enactment of good laws.

The most uncontestable instances of bad law must be those that flourish in totalitarian societies. It may be possible to imagine a modern dictatorial regime in which the constraints of the rule of law are meticulously observed, but such a phenomenon exists only in the realms of fiction. In all of the most oppressive regimes of the present century, legality values, particularly in the areas of ordinary and political crimes, were not simply ignored but were, in fact, deliberately and systematically destroyed. We may trust such regimes to identify what is essential to their own existence, and the lesson they teach is that massive assaults on the values of greatest importance to liberal societies will be preceded by extinction of the legality ideal. It also may be observed that the forms of law sometimes appear to be made of more durable stuff than its substantive content. History provides more than one instance of the persistence of legal forms and institutions making possible the rebirth of a regime of rights after a period of harsh authoritarian rule in which the substantive protections of law had been largely eliminated. Something approaching this phenomenon may recently have occurred in the Republic of South Africa when the existing courts and a long tradition of statutory interpretation appear to have initiated virtually the only checks on the exercise of rampant executive power operating within the governmental apparatus.[2] The flourishing of rights in the Glorious Revolution of the seventeenth century was anchored on legal forms, many of which were in existence during the repressive Tudor and Stuart dynasties. Those committed to the serving of basic substantive rights through the agency of law cannot prudently neglect strengthening the forms of legality and resisting contemporary assaults on it.

But contributions of the rule of law to the making of good laws are not confined to extreme situations involving the possibilities or actuality of totalitarian rule. In the course of ordinary lawmaking, close adherence to the forms of legality tends to the increased rationality of law and therefore to the production of laws that are substantively good. The assertion deserves a more extended and systematic development than can be given here. A single illustration will be offered. Central to the legality ideal is the requirement that laws be articulated with a clarity and generality sufficient to strengthen the capacities of citizens for self-direction and to discourage capricious and arbitrary uses of public authority by officials. These values are indispensable to liberal societies. But the requirement of careful articulation contributes other virtues. The very effort to state a legal proposition clearly and comprehensively may often uncover aspects and complexities not at first apparent, providing opportunities for a fuller and more effective response to the problems for which substantive solutions are sought through the processes of lawmaking. Careful articulation may also lessen avoidable conflicts and inconsistencies among new and existing laws and hence diminishes dissonance and incoherence within the total corpus of the law. It follows that slighting the obligation of careful articulation at the legislative, judicial, or administrative levels lessens the rationality and effectiveness of law and often results in the creation of bad laws.

It cannot be expected that the importance of the search for a more lawful law will always be widely understood or appreciated within the community. This is not because the American public is indifferent to the claims of legality. On the contrary, from the beginning of our national identity, the ideal of a government of laws has exerted potent influences on the theory of our political institutions and has contributed much that is most attractive to our public life. There seems no reason to doubt that threats to the rule of law, when widely perceived and understood, will continue to evoke public concern and response. In the welter of a complex and contentious society, however, legality issues may be obscured or overriden by apparently more pressing concerns. Public attention will ordinarily and understandably be engaged by such purposes as diminishing the threat of private violence, enlarging the availability of medical care, or achieving economic security for an uncertain future. The community's interests in public measures clearly directed to improving the conditions of life will ordinarily be strong, but understanding of and concerns about the means by which the law can best achieve its social purposes must be supplied initially and in larger part by legally trained persons. In the generation just past, lawyers, on the whole, have not made strengthening the legality ideal in American society an objective of central concern; nor have they adequately communicated to the larger community the importance of such revitalization. The dangers of neglect, however, are becoming increasingly evident. The present realities provide a basis for hope that American lawyers, both those in practice and in the academy, may be moved to encompass reinvigoration of the habits of legality within the urgent obligations of professional responsibility.

Notes

Chapter 1. The Intellectual Environment of Legality

1. It is asserted that although Dicey popularized the phrase, he did not originate it. Arndt, *The Origins of Dicey's Concept of "The Rule of Law,"* 31 AUST. L.J. 117 (1937). Dicey's career is reviewed in R. COSGROVE, THE RULE OF LAW: ALBERT VENN DICEY (1980). *See* A. V. DICEY, INTRODUCTION TO THE STUDY OF THE LAW OF THE CONSTITUTION 202–03 (10th ed.) 1960.

2. The concept was given expression in the popular literature of ancient Athens. A character in a play by Euripides asserts that nothing is more hostile to a city than a despot. But, he continues, "[W]hen the laws are written down, rich and poor alike have equal justice, and it is open to the weaker to use the same language to the prosperous when he is reviled by him, and the weaker prevails over the stronger if he has justice on his side." THE SUPPLIANTS (E. Coleridge trans.), *in* 5 GREAT BOOKS OF THE WESTERN WORLD 258, 262 (1952) [hereinafter GREAT BOOKS]. For a brief survey of the history of the idea in Greek thought with emphasis on the term *isonomy,* see F. A. HAYEK, THE POLITICAL IDEAL OF THE RULE OF LAW 6–7 (1955); *see also* C. BOWRA, THE GREEK EXPERIENCE 78–79 (1957).

3. ARISTOTLE, POLITICS (B. Jowett trans.) (bk. III, ch. 16, 1287a), *in* 9 GREAT BOOKS, *supra* note 2, at 445, 485.

4. Weinreb, *The Intelligibility of the Rule of Law, in* THE RULE OF LAW: IDEAL OR IDEOLOGY 59–60 (Hutchinson & Monahan eds.) (1987).

5. "[§(39)] No free man shall be seized or imprisoned, or stripped of his rights or possessions, or outlawed or exiled, or

deprived of his standing in any other way, nor will we proceed with force against him, or send others to do so, except by the lawful judgement of his equals or by the law of the land." L. WRIGHT, MAGNA CARTA AND THE TRADITION OF LIBERTY 56 (1976).

6. "Let him [the King], therefore, temper his power by law, which is the bridle of power, that he may live according to the laws, for the law of mankind has decreed that his own laws bind the lawgiver . . . . [I]t is a saying worthy of the majesty of a ruler that the prince acknowledges himself bound by the laws." 2 BRACTON, ON THE LAWS AND CUSTOMS OF ENGLAND 305–06 (S. Thorne trans., 1968).

7. "In the modern world, general human liberty, as distinguished from the liberties that are privileges of the few, hardly existed before the England of the seventeenth century." F. HAYEK, *supra* note 2, at 5.

8. The historian Jules Michelet describes the beginnings of the French Revolution as *"l'avenement de la loi."* 1 HISTOIRE DE LA REVOLUTION FRANÇAISE xxiii, *quoted in* F. HAYEK, *supra* note 2, at 17.

9. AN ESSAY ON CRIMES AND PUNISHMENTS (Academic Reprints, 1953) (2d Am. ed. 1819). Early in the essay, Beccaria says, "I should have every thing to fear if tyrants were to read my book; but tyrants never read." *Id.* at 26.

10. The statement in the text, of course, does not attempt a full statement of the rule-of-law concept. *Cf.* Summers, *A Formal Theory of the Rule of Law,* 6 RATIO JURIS 127, 129 (1993): "The ideal of the rule of law consists essentially of the authorized governance of at least basic social relations between citizens and between citizens and their government so far as feasible through published formal rules congruently interpreted and applied, with the officialdom itself subject to rules defining the manner and limits of their activity, and with sanctions and other redress against citizens and officials for departures from rules being imposed only by impartial and independent courts or by similar tribunals, after due notice and opportunity for hearing."

11. Thus F.A. Hayek formulated the rule of law as follows: "Stripped of all technicalities this means that the government in all its actions is bound by rules fixed and announced beforehand— rules which make it possible to foresee with fair certainty how the authority will make use of its coercive powers in given circumstances and to plan one's individual affairs on the basis of this knowledge." ROAD TO SERFDOM 72 (1944). John Stuart Mill refers to "that government of law, which is the foundation of all modern life . . . ." REPRESENTATIVE GOVERNMENT ch. 2, *in* 43 GREAT BOOKS, *supra* note 2, at 339.

12. One of the contested definitional issues in the rule-of-law literature concerns whether the concept should be limited to the formal aspects of law or whether it must be seen to include certain basic substantive rights, particularly those of political participation. Strong arguments have been marshaled for the restricted definition. Including elements of the substantive content of laws in the concept's definition is seen as a source of confusion and an obstacle to coherent analysis. Moreover, identifying the rule of law with basic individual rights may result in neglect of the formal aspects of law and in slighting its systemic applications. If substantive rights are deemed part of the concept, consensus on what is to be included may be difficult or impossible to achieve. Raz, *The Rule of Law and Its Virtue,* 93 LAW Q. REV. 195 (1977); Summers, *The Ideal Socio-Legal Order: Its "Rule of Law" Dimension,* 1 RATIO JURIS 154 (1988).

The tendency toward the imperialistic expansion of the rule-of-law idea is well illustrated by INTERNATIONAL CONGRESS OF JURISTS, THE RULE OF LAW IN A FREE SOCIETY issued in 1959 at New Dehi. The Delhi Report, as it has come to be known, equates the rule of law with fulfillment of virtually all human needs and aspirations; in effect, it includes within the concept an agenda for a socialist society. *See* REPORT cl. 1 (1959). Such efforts to identify the rule of law with so wide a range of objectives, most of which remain hotly disputed in the arenas of democratic politics, deprives the rule of law of specific meaning and denies it important support from many groups and constituencies. Allen, *A Crisis of Legality in the Criminal Law? Reflections on the Rule of Law,* 42 MERCER L. REV. 811, 819 (1991).

Maintaining independence of the rule-of-law concept from the broad areas of substantive rights may be easier to achieve in political societies that have traditionally afforded them strong protection. In the politics of developing nations and societies emerging from totalitarian rule, however, the linkage of the rule of law to at least some basic individual rights and immunities may be a practical necessity. A rule of law may have small appeal for a population recently oppressed by the law, or by what passed for law, of a tyrannical regime unless the rule of law is viewed as integral to a panoply of human rights. *See* A. MATHEWS, FREEDOM, SECURITY, AND THE RULE OF LAW 13 (1986). Note also the linkage between the rule-of-law concept and the "substantive" principle of penal proportion, discussed in *infra* chapter 2, at note 99.

13. THE SPIRIT OF LAWS, *in* 38 GREAT BOOKS, *supra* note 2, at 1, 85.

14. *Cf.* Summers, *Theory, Formality, and Practical Legal Criticism,* 106 Law Q. Rev. 407 (1990).

15. *Cf.* T. Honderich, Political Violence 1 (1976): "We can only agree that all of philosophy, in order to come within sight of its several ends, must have far less to do with empirical fact than those disciplines which have its discovery and explanation as their only end. However, in the political philosophy which implicitly or explicitly recommends action to us, or more likely inaction, premises of empirical fact necessarily have a larger importance than elsewhere in philosophy."

16. Dicey, *supra* note 1, at 195.

17. Aristotle, *supra* note 3, at 512; *see also* Shklar, *Political Theory and the Rule of Law, in* The Rule of Law: Ideal or Ideology, *supra* note 4, at 1, 6.

18. Krygier, *Marxism and the Rule of Law: Reflections After the Collapse of Communism,* 15 Law & Soc. Inquiry 633 (1990).

19. *Cf.* F. Zimring, The Changing Legal World of Adolescence 159 (1982).

20. H.L.A. Hart, The Concept of Law 135 (1961).

21. Allen, *Nineteen Eighty-Four and the Eclipse of Private Worlds, in* The Future of Nineteen Eighty-Four (E. Jensen ed.) (1984).

22. The most effective statement of the point is that made in M. Kadish & S. Kadish, Discretion To Disobey viii (1973).

23. P. Atiyah & R. Summers, Form and Substance in Anglo-American Law (1987).

24. Kadish & Kadish, *supra* note 22, at viii.

25. Allen, *The Morality of Means: Three Problems in Criminal Sanctions,* 42 U. Pitt. L. Rev. 737, 740 (1980).

26. *See, e.g.,* M. White, Social Thought in America: The Revolt Against Formalism (1964).

27. *See supra* note 6.

28. In the first edition of his widely read work, The Bramble Bush 3, 5 (1930), Llewellyn stated that "what . . . officials do about disputes is, to my mind, the law itself." He continued, "[R]ules are important so far as they help you . . . predict what judges will do . . . . That is all their importance, except as pretty playthings." Twenty-one years later he commented that these "are unhappy words when not more fully developed, and they are plainly at best a very partial statement of the whole truth . . . . [O]ne office of law is to control officials in some part, and to guide them . . . where no thoroughgoing control is possible, or is desired . . . . [T]he words fail to take proper account . . . of the

office of the institution of law as an instrument of conscious shaping . . . ." (2d ed. 1951), at 9.

29. LAW AND THE MODERN MIND (1930).

30. *Cf.* Schauer, *Formalities,* 97 YALE L.J. 509, 530–32 (1988).

31. Krygier, *supra* note 18, at 640.

32. H. ADAMS, THE EDUCATION OF HENRY ADAMS 451 (1918, 1931).

33. "Bentham's detailed concern with language and his sense of it as a source of mystification, and the need for what has been called the 'nettoyage de la situation verbale' as the essential accompaniment of any serious study, is one of the features of Bentham's thought which distinguishes him from thinkers of the European enlightenment from which he drew much inspiration." H.L.A. HART, ESSAYS ON BENTHAM 2 (1982).

34. *E.g.,* 2 J. BENTHAM, BOOK OF FALLACIES, *in* THE WORKS OF JEREMY BENTHAM 438, 441 (J. Bowring ed.) (1962).

35. "Bentham's attack inspired the great statutory reforms of the law of evidence of 1843, 1851, and 1898, which, as the lawyers who lived through these changes said, amounted almost to a legal revolution." HART, *supra* note 33, at 31.

36. For a sophisticated expression of this position, see Frug, *Henry James, Lee Marvin, and the Law,* N.Y. TIMES BOOK REVIEW, Feb. 16, 1986, at 1, 28.

37. The significance of the past for social reform is addressed in H. MARCUSE, ONE-DIMENSIONAL MAN 98–99 (1964): "Remembrance of the past may give rise to dangerous insights, and the established society seems to be apprehensive of the subversive contents of memory. Remembrance is a mode of disassociation from the given facts, a mode of 'mediation' which breaks, for short moments, the omnipresent power of the given facts. Memory recalls the terror and the hope that passed. Both come to life again, but whereas in reality the former recurs in ever new forms, the latter remains hope. And in the personal events which reappear in the individual memory, the fears and aspirations of mankind assert themselves—the universal in the particular."

38. *Cf.* Frug, *supra* note 36, at 1: "[M]ore and more lawyers these days recognize that the law can be read the way one reads literature, and they are using works of literature and the techniques of modern literary theory to explain and analyze the subject."

39. *Cf.* Vining, *Generalization in Interpretative Theory* 6, REPRESENTATIONS (Spring 1990): "[A]s a lawyer one reads for the purpose of oneself making a statement of law for which one is respon-

sible. Lawyers in the schools make their statements to students or the world at large; in administration or in what is commonly designated as the practice of law lawyers make their statements to client or commission or, acting as judges or attorneys general, to the world at large."

40. *Id.* at 4.

41. *Cf.* Summers & Marshall, *The Argument from Ordinary Meaning in Statutory Interpretation,* 43 N. IRELAND LEGAL Q. 215, 224–225 (1992).

42. R. UNGER, LAW AND MODERN SOCIETY *passim* (1976).

43. Allen, *Remembering* Shelley v. Kraemer: *Of Public and Private Worlds,* 67 WASH. U. L.Q. 709, 729–32 (1989).

44. L. FULLER, THE MORALITY OF LAW 39 (rev. ed.) (1969) ("Certainly there can be no rational ground for asserting that a man can have a moral obligation to obey a legal rule that does not exist, or is kept secret from him, or that came into existence only after he had acted, or was unintelligible, or was contradicted by another rule of the same system, or command the impossible, or changed every minute."); F. HAYAK, *supra* note 2, at 33.

45. The *nulla poena* principle is ordinarily bracketed with the companion proposition, *Nullum crimen sine lege.* For the purposes of this discussion, delineation of distinctions between the two propositions seems unnecessary. *Nulla poena* has attracted a substantial literature. *E.g.,* J. HALL, GENERAL PRINCIPLES OF CRIMINAL LAW 27–70 (2d ed. 1960); Elliot, *Nulla Poena Sine Lege,* 1 JURID. REV. 22 (1956); Glazer, *Nullum Crimen Sine Lege,* 24 J. COMP. LEGIS. & INT'L. L. 28 (3d ser. 1942); Hall, *Nulla Poena Sine Lege,* 47 YALE L.J. 165 (1937); Zupancic, *On Legal Formalism: The Principle of Legality in Criminal Law,* 27 LOY. L. REV. 369 (1981).

46. One of the most arresting modern discussions of the principle that bars ex post facto adjudication in criminal cases, including its possible limitations, is to be found in the famous debate between H.L.A. Hart and Lon Fuller. *See* Hart, *Positivism and the Separation of Law and Morals,* 71 HARV. L. REV. 593, 618–20 (1958); Fuller, *Positivism and Fidelity to Law, id.* at 630, 649–61. As would be expected, the Nazi regime made extensive use of ex post facto prosecutions, even in capital cases. Thus, Ingo Müller cites the case of Joseph C, a Jew, who was sentenced to death by a Hamburg special court for behavior that occurred three months before the decree in question took effect. The decree expressly authorized prosecutions of crimes committed before its promulgation. HITLER'S JUSTICE 135 (D. Schneider trans.) (1991); *see also id.* at 33–34.

47. Summers, *supra* note 12, at 160.

48. The views of the Italian school of criminology, especially those of Cesare Lombroso and Raffaele Garofalo, are pertinent here. *See* F. ALLEN, *Garofalo's Criminology and Some Modern Problems, in* THE BORDERLAND OF CRIMINAL JUSTICE 63–90 (1964).

49. *The General Theory of Law and Marxism, in* PASHUKANIS: SELECTED WRITINGS ON MARXISM AND LAW 89 (P. Bierne & R. SHARLET eds.) (1980), *quoted in* Krygier, *supra* note 18, at 656. Similar expressions can be found in Nazi jurisprudential writing. Thus, in Müller, *supra* note 46, at 154: "Furthermore, the methods developed by Nazi jurists, in particular the doctrine of 'criminal types' and 'teleological interpretation' allowed the courts to dispense with fine distinctions about how the law defined a particular crime and whether the act committed actually fulfilled these requirements." *See also id.* at 79.

50. *Cf.* HALL, *supra* note 45, at 54.

51. F. ALLEN, THE DECLINE OF THE REHABILITATIVE IDEAL 32–59 (1981).

52. *E.g.,* Internal Security Act, No. 74 of 1982 (Stat. Rep. S. Afr.).

53. See discussions in MÜLLER, *supra* note 46, and H. KOCH, IN THE NAME OF THE VOLK (1989).

54. KOCH, *supra* note 53, at 16, 213.

55. The German Act provided: "Any person who commits an act which the law declares to be punishable or which is deserving of penalty according to the fundamental conceptions of a penal law and sound popular feeling, shall be punished. If there is no penal law directly covering an act it shall be punished under the law of which the fundamental conception applies most nearly to the said act." The Russian Code of 1926, R.S.F.S.R. Penal Code, art. II-6, stated: "A crime is any socially dangerous act or omission which threatens the foundations of the Soviet political structure and the system of law which has been established by the Workers' and Peasants' Government for the period of transition to a communist structure." *Quoted in* Zupancic, *supra* note 45, at 411 n.99; *see also* HALL, GENERAL PRINCIPLES OF CRIMINAL LAW, *supra* note 45, at 66–67. The open-endedness of the Canadian Constitutional Act, 1982, Pt. 1, §11(g), REV. STATUTES OF CANADA, Appendix II, no. 44 (1985) is surprising: "Any person charged with an offence has the right . . . (g) not to be found guilty of any act or omission unless, at the time of the act or omission, it constituted an offence under Canadian *or international law or was criminal according to the general principles of law recognized by the community of nations."* (Emphasis supplied)

56. FULLER, *supra* note 44; *see* Justice Hugo Black's dis-

sent in Ginsburg v. United States, 383 U.S. 463, 447 (1966): "[B]ad governments either wrote no general rules of conduct at all, leaving that highly important task to the unbridled discretion of government agents at the moment of trial, or sometimes, as history tells us, wrote their laws in unknown tongues so that people could not understand them or else placed their written laws at such inaccessible spots that people could not read them."

57. In his seminal work, THE SOCIETY OF CAPTIVES 74–75 (1958), Gresham Sykes found that, at the time of writing, prison rules were often incomprehensible, explanations for administrative action withheld, and lack of understanding by the prison populations often deliberately fostered. "Indeed, the incomprehensible order or rule is a basic feature of life in prison." *Id.* at 74. Since that time written rules available to the prisoners have become the norm in most American prison systems. Questions of vagueness and comprehensibility of regulations remain, however. Babcock, *Due Process in Prison Disciplinary Proceedings,* 22 B.C. L. REV. 1009 (1981). Certain penal institutions appear to have been particularly slow to reform methods of communication to the inmate populations and explanations of the grounds for disciplinary measures. Lyden & Schiller, *The Prison That Defies Reform,* 15 STUDENT LAW. 9 (1987); HOUSE SUBCOMM. ON COURTS, CIVIL LIBERTIES, AND THE ADMINISTRATION OF JUSTICE, OVERSIGHT HEARING: MARION PRISON, 1985 SERIAL NO. 26 (June 26, 1985). A considerable literature exists on these and related issues. *See, e.g.,* J. DILUTIO, COURTS, CORRECTIONS, AND THE CONSTITUTION (1990).

58. Peters & Norris, *Reconsidering Parole Release Decisions in Illinois: Facts, Myths, and the Need for Policy Changes,* 24 MARQ. L. REV. 815, 822 (1991) ("The Board has frequently been criticized for paying too little attention to its reasons for denying parole. Too often the Board lumps vastly different inmates into the same category or treats similarly situated inmates differently."); Wile, *An Overview of the Parole Revocation Process in Pennsylvania,* 92 DICK. L. REV. 1, 53 (1987) ("The Pennsylvania Commonwealth Court has often criticized the Parole Board for its 'cryptic' revocation decisions."); *see also* N. COHEN & J. GOBERT, THE LAW OF PROBATION AND PAROLE (1983).

59. Thus, in a particularly appealing case for exculpation on grounds of mistake of law, the Court of Appeals of New York denied the defense on the ground that to accept it would "create legal chaos." People v. Marrero, 69 N.Y.2d 382, 389, 507 N.E.2d 1068, 1071 (1987). The court did not point to any historical experience to support its prediction. The conservatism of the American Law In-

stitute on these issues is one of its least attractive features. *See* MODEL PENAL CODE § 2.04(3) (1962). A much more hospitable reception to the mistake-of-law doctrine is typical of the legal systems of Western Europe. *See, e.g.,* Ryu & Silving, *Error Juris: A Comparative Survey,* 24 U. CHI. L. REV. 421 (1957).

60. A brief history of the doctrine of judicial independence may be found in W. SPECK, STABILITY AND STRIFE: ENGLAND 1714–1760, at 12–13 (1977). *See also Basic Principles on the Independence of the Judiciary* (United Nations, Aug. 1988).

61. *Quoted in* MÜLLER, *supra* note 46, at 192; *see also id.* at 73.

62. Allen, *A Serendipitous Trek Through the Advance-Sheet Jungle: Criminal Justice in the Courts of Review,* 70 IOWA L. REV. 311, 316–17 (1985); Allen, *A Crisis of Legality in the Criminal Law? Reflections on the Rule of Law,* 42 MERCER L. REV. 811, 815 (1991).

63. FULLER, *supra* note 44, at 39.

64. *E.g.,* BECCARIA, *supra* note 9, at 23–24.

65. Klein, *The Eleventh Commandment: Thou Shalt Not Be Compelled To Render the Ineffective Assistance of Counsel,* 68 IND. L.J. 363 (1993) ("As the number of indigents charged with crimes has increased, in part due to expanded funding for police and prosecutors to fight the national and local 'war on drugs,' there has not been a corresponding increase of funding to provide counsel for indigent defendants. In fact, due to widespread financial difficulties impacting local and state governments the money available for court-appointed counsel and public defenders has actually declined in many localities."); Lardent & Cohen, *The Last Best Hope: Representing Death Row Inmates,* 23 LOY. L.A. L. REV. 213, 214 (1989) ("The reality of appointed counsel for indigent defendants at trial and on direct appeal is that these attorneys are often inadequately compensated, unaware of the complex procedure and jurisprudence in capital cases, novices in the practice of law, and unable to obtain critically needed support services such as investigators and expert witnesses.").

66. POVERTY AND THE ADMINISTRATION OF FEDERAL CRIMINAL JUSTICE (Report of the Attorney General's Committee on Poverty and the Administration of Criminal Justice) 10–11 (1963): "The essence of the adversary system is challenge. The survival of our system of criminal justice and the values which it advances depends on a constant, searching, and creative questioning of official decisions and assertions of authority at all stages of the process. The proper performance of the defense function is thus as vital to the health of the system as the performance of the prosecuting and adjudicatory functions. It follows that insofar as the financial status of the accused impedes vigorous and proper chal-

lenges, it constitutes a threat to the viability of the adversary system. We believe that the system is imperilled by the large numbers of accused persons unable to employ counsel or to meet even modest bail requirements . . . . The loss to the interests of accused individuals, occasioned by these failures, are great and apparent . . . . Beyond these considerations, however, is the fact that the conditions produced by the financial incapacity of the accused are detrimental to the proper functioning of the system of justice and that the loss of vitality of the adversary system, thereby occasioned, significantly endangers the basic interests of a free community."

67. Müller *supra* note 46, at 64.

68. *Id.*

69. *Id.* at 64.

70. George, *Discretionary Authority of Public Prosecutors in Japan*, 17 Law in Japan 42, 72 (1984): "Thus, the chief controls on abusive exercise of prosecutorial authority in Japan flow from professional, traditional, and administrative standards, not external and judicial."

71. *Cf.* Christie, *An Essay on Discretion*, 1986 Duke L.J. 747, 754–55.

72. S. Chorover, From Genesis to Genocide 9 (1979); R.J. Lifton, The Nazi Doctors: Medical Killing and the Psychology of Genocide (1986); Szasz, *Soviet Psychiatry: Its Supporters*, Inquiry 4–5 (Jan. 2, 1978).

73. Allen, *supra* note 51, *passim.*

74. Hart, *supra* note 20, at 123, 128–29.

75. *Cf.* Alschuler, *The Failure of Sentencing Guidelines: A Plea for Less Aggregation*, 58 U. Chi. L. Rev. 901, 939–49 (1991).

76. *E.g.*, 18 U.S.C. § 242 (1948).

77. Fuller, *supra* note 44, at 39.

78. *A Juster Justice, A More Lawful Law, in* Essays in Honor of O.K. Murray 537–64 (1927).

79. Model Penal Code art. 3, § 3.02 (1980).

80. The statement continues: "It Is Always Unknown; It Is Different In Different Men; It Is Casual And Depends Upon Constitution, Temper, And Passion; In The Best It Is Oftentimes Caprice; In The Worst It Is Every Vice, Folly And Passion To Which Human Nature Is Liable." *Quoted in* Pound, *Discretion, Dispensation, and Mitigation: The Problem of the Individual Special Case*, 35 N.Y.U. L. Rev. 925, 926 (1960).

81. Traité de Droit Constitutionel 681 (3d ed.) (Paris 1927), *quoted in* Kadish & Kadish, *supra* note 22, at 42.

82. Dicey, *supra* note 1, at 202. The meaning of the rule of law

is said to encompass, in part, "the absolute supremacy or predominance of regular law as opposed to the influence of arbitrary power, and excludes the existence of arbitrariness, of prerogative, or even of wide discretionary authority on the part of government."

83. The influential STRUGGLE FOR JUSTICE (American Friend's Service Committee, 1971) may serve as an example.

84. The point is elaborated in ALLEN, *supra* note 51, at 87–88.

85. KADISH & KADISH, *supra* note 22.

86. It should not be overlooked, however, that highly important work has been done. *E.g.*, K. DAVIS, DISCRETIONARY JUSTICE (1962); POLICE DISCRETION (1975). The emphasis of the American Bar Foundation's *Survey of the Administration of Criminal Justice in the United States* in the mid-1950s on identifying the critical decisions made at the various stages of the criminal process has thrown important light on the nature and significance of discretion in the criminal process and has inspired a legacy of important empirical and theoretical work.

87. A useful development of the point is presented in Vorenberg, *Narrowing the Discretion of Criminal Justice Officials,* 1976 DUKE L.J. 651.

88. 1–3 AMERICAN LAW INSTITUTE, MODEL PENAL CODE AND COMMENTARIES (1980); *see* Symposium: *The 25th Anniversary of the Model Penal Code,* 19 RUTGERS L.J. 519–954 (1988).

Chapter 2. The Institutional Environment of Legality

1. L. MASUR, RITES OF EXECUTION AND THE TRANSFORMATION OF AMERICAN CULTURE, 1776–1865 (1989).

2. W. LEWIS, FROM NEWGATE TO DANNEMORA 64–65 (Ithaca: 1965); Allen, *Central Problems of American Criminal Justice,* 75 MICH. L. REV. 813 (1977). A probably unfounded impression of a crime crisis in late-nineteenth-century Europe has been identified as one motivating factor in the attack on classical criminology and the rise of positivist schools of criminology of that period. McClain, *Introduction* to C. LOMBROSO, CRIME: ITS CAUSES AND REMEDIES 11n.18 (1994).

3. PRESIDENT'S COMM'N ON LAW ENFORCEMENT & THE ADMIN. OF JUST., THE CHALLENGE OF CRIME IN A FREE SOCIETY (1967); *see also* Radzinowicz, *Penal Regressions,* 50 CAMBRIDGE L. J. 422, 431 (1991).

4. The recommendations of the Commission made tangible contributions to professionalizing the police, advancing criminal

justice education, and promoting corrections as a field for training and research.

5. *Cf.* Radzinowicz, *supra* note 3, at 431.

6. F. ALLEN, THE CRIMES OF POLITICS 13–14 (1974).

7. "The machinery is simply breaking up in its crucial components under the sheer weight of numbers. Nor should one be surprised to note that the chronic 'crime pressure' inevitably also leads to a crystallisation of public opinion against measures of criminal policy inspired by a liberal social outlook usually identified with authoritarian systems of criminal justice." Radzinowicz, *supra* note 3, at 425.

8. BUREAU OF JUST. STATS., U.S. DEP'T OF JUST., SOURCEBOOK OF CRIMINAL JUSTICE STATISTICS—1993, at 353 table 3.108 (1994) [hereinafter SOURCEBOOK—1993].

9. *Id.*

10. *Id.*, 418 table 4.1. "Violent crimes" include "murder, forcible rape, robbery, and aggravated assault." "Property crimes" include "burglary, larceny-theft, motor vehicle theft, and arson."

11. In 1992, 23% of U.S. households were reported victimized by a crime of violence or theft, and 5% of all households had at least one member 12 years or older who was a victim of a violent crime. The figures for black and Hispanic households are higher. BUREAU OF JUST. STATS., U.S. DEP'T OF JUST., HIGHLIGHTS FROM 20 YEARS OF SURVEYING CRIME VICTIMS NCJ-144525, at 6 (Oct. 1993) [herein after HIGHLIGHTS].

12. BUREAU OF JUST. STATS., U.S. DEP'T OF JUST., *Prisons in 1992,* at 2 (May 1993) [hereinafter PRISONS IN 1992].

13. *Id.*

14. The average daily jail population in 1992 was stated to be 444,584. SOURCEBOOK—1993 *supra* note 8, at 591 table 6.17.

15. BUREAU OF JUST. STATS., U.S. DEP'T OF JUST., SOURCEBOOK OF CRIMINAL JUST. STATS.—1992 [hereinafter SOURCEBOOK—1992] as of January 1, 1990, there were 2,521,525 probationers in the United States. *Id.* at 567 table 6.2. The parole population on the same date was 456,803. *Id.* at 659 table 6.112. For the populations of American states as determined by the 1990 census, see U.S. DEP'T. OF COM., STATISTICAL ABSTRACT OF THE UNITED STATES—1992.

16. Baum, *Tunnel Vision: The War on Drugs, 12 Years Later,* 79 A.B.A. J. 70, 71 (1993). It is said that the figure approaches 50% in the cities of Washington and Baltimore. *See also* Bender, *Crime and Punishment in the 1990s: Solution or Illusion?,* 5 CRIM. JUST. (Fall 1990) ("[I]n 1986, there were more young black men under the arm of the criminal justice system, than the total number of

black males of all ages enrolled in college."). On the vulnerability of black males as victims of homicide, see Gibbs, *The Social Context of Teenage Pregnancy and Parenting, in* PARENTHOOD AND COMING OF AGE IN THE 1990s at 78 (M. Rosenheim & M. Testa eds.) (1992) [hereinafter PARENTHOOD] ("A young black male has a one in twenty-one chance of being murdered before he reaches age twenty-one, usually by another black male who fires a gun. . . . Young black males are six times more likely as white males to be victims of homicide."); *see also* Bastian & Taylor, U.S. DEP'T OF JUST. YOUNG BLACK MALE VICTIMS, (Crime Data Brief) (Dec. 1994).

17. Radzinowicz, *supra* note 3, at 439–43.

18. COUNCIL OF EUROPE, PRISON INFORMATION BULLETIN 29 table 2 (June 1992). In fact, somewhat higher rates were reported in the same publication for Northern Ireland and Hungary.

19. PRISONS IN 1992, *supra* note 12. Since the international statistics include both prison and jail populations, the comparable figure for the United States is well over 400 per 100,000 inhabitants. (U.S. BUREAU OF JUST. STATS., U.S. DEP'T OF JUST., SOURCEBOOK OF CRIMINAL JUSTICE STATISTICS—1990 AT 610–1990, AT 610 table 6.60 (1991) [hereinafter SOURCEBOOK–1990].

20. SOURCEBOOK—1990, *supra* note 19, at 609 table 6.59; PRISON INFORMATION BULLETIN, *supra* note 18, at 29 table 2.

21. U.S. BUREAU OF JUST. STATS., U.S. DEP'T OF JUST., SOURCEBOOK OF CRIMINAL JUSTICE STATS.—1991, at 394 table 3.134 (1992) [hereinafter SOURCEBOOK—1991]; INTERPOL, INTERNATIONAL CRIME STATISTICS, 1989–1990 (1992).

22. *Business International: Country Profile* (Nov. 9, 1992).

23. SOURCEBOOK—1993, *supra* note 8, at 494 table 5.22.

24. Another cause of the expanding criminal dockets of federal courts is the increasing federalization of American criminal law, the congressional practice of defining as federal crimes, conduct that theretofore had been left to the exclusive concern of the states. Chief Justice William Rehnquist has characterized the continuing development as a "serious drain on the [federal] judiciary's resources." *Seen in the Glass Darkly: The Future of the Federal Courts,* 1993 WIS. L. REV. 1, 7.

25. Insofar as pertinent to present purposes, the Speedy Trial Act of 1974 provides: "In any case in which a plea of not guilty is entered, the trial of a defendant charged under information or indictment with the commission of an offense shall commence within seventy days of the filing date . . . of the information or indictment, or from the date the defendant has appeared before a judicial officer of the court in which such charge is pending,

whichever last occurs . . ." 18 U.S.C, § 3161(c)(l) (1975) "If the defendant is not brought to trial within [the required time limit], the information shall be dismissed on motion of the defendant." *Id.* § 3162(c).

26. *Report* (Hon. Joseph F. Weis, Jr., Chairman) (Apr. 2, 1990) at 36. The Federal Courts Study Committee was appointed by the Chief Justice of the United States at the direction of Congress. See Pub. L. no. 100–702, 102 Stat. 4642 (1988). Similar expressions of concern have been frequent: *See Proceedings of the Fifty-Second Judicial Conference of the District of Columbia Circuit* 140 F.R.D. 481, 589 (June 5–7, 1991); Wisotsky, *A Nation of Suspects: The War on Drugs and Civil Liberties* 21 (No. 180 Policy Analysis, Cato Inst., Oct. 2, 1992) ("[I]n many districts the crush of drug cases . . . was so great that the adjudication of ordinary civil cases had virtually ceased.").

27. Lavelle, *"It's Safer To Cheat,"* Nat'l L. Rev. 1, 2 (1990).

28. *Id.*

29. *Redirecting Criminal Tax Enforcement To Improve Voluntary Compliance,* A.B.A. Tax Sec. Comm. on Civil & Crim. Tax Penalties (May 28, 1991). *See also* 91 Tax Notes Today (Tax Analysts) 177–14 (Aug. 23, 1991). In response to these and similar criticisms, the Commissioner of Internal Revenue appointed a study group and ultimately concluded that "there should be no changes" in the IRS's enforcement policy. 92 Tax Notes Today (Tax Analysts) 9–53 (Jan. 14, 1992).

30. *See* 1 Federal Courts Study Comm., Working Papers and Subcommittee Reports 26 table 2, 27 table 3 (June 1, 1990). It should be noted, however, that certain categories of civil litigation increased at even higher rates. *Id.* at 26.

31. "For example, in several trials involving hotly contested issues of insanity, prosecutors have gone before juries and implied that defendants will be 'let go' if the insanity defense prevails, making no mention of the very likely compulsory hospital commitments of the defendants in the event of their acquittals on insanity grounds. The conclusion of a Tennessee appellate court, for example, that such jury argument was 'entirely harmless' seems surprisingly assured at a time when the insanity defense is widely (even if undeservedly) believed to be a major threat to the security of the community from acts of criminal violence." Allen, *A Serendipitous Trek Through the Advance-Sheet Jungle: Criminal Justice in the Courts of Review,* 70 Iowa L. Rev. 311, 331 (1985) (citing State v. Estes, 655 S.W.2d 179, 185 (Tenn. Crim. App. 1983)).

32. Davies, *Affirmed: A Study of Criminal Appeals and Decision*

Making Norms in a California Court of Appeals, 1982 AM. B. FOUND. RES. J. 543.

33. Barclay v. Florida, 463 U.S. 939, 988 (1983) (Marshall, J., dissenting).

34. For a particularly insightful essay on these matters, see Fuller, *The Adversary Process, in* TALKS ON AMERICAN LAW (H. Berman ed.) (1961). "The purpose of the rule is to preserve the integrity of society itself. It aims at keeping sound and wholesome procedures by which society visits its condemnation on an erring member . . . . The lawyer appearing on behalf of an accused person is not present in court merely to represent his client. He represents a vital interest of society itself, he plays an essential role in one of the fundamental processes of an ordered community." *Id.* at 39, 41. The wider importance of the human rights lawyer in the authoritarian society of South Africa may be gleaned from S. ELLMAN, IN A TIME OF TROUBLE (1992). *See especially id.* at 274 *et seq.*

35. *See supra* note 66 and accompanying text in chapter 1.

36. *See supra* notes 67, 68 and accompanying text in chapter 1.

37. 287 U.S. 45 (1932); *see also* Johnson v. Zerbst, 304 U.S. 458 (1938); *cf.* Arrango, *Tennessee Indigent Defender System in Crisis,* CRIM. JUST. 42, Spring 1992. For an account of the impact of the "war on drugs" on the quality of defense services afforded indigents accused in the federal courts, see Finkelman, *The Second Casuality of War: Civil Liberties and the War on Drugs,* 66 S. CAL L. REV. 1389, 1440–44 (1993).

38. The general criteria are stated in United States v. Cromic, 466 U.S. 648 (1984), and Strickland v. Washington, 466 U.S. 668 (1984). The test to be met by the accused, as stated in the former case, is a showing on the part of the accused that there was "an actual breakdown of the adversary process." Cromic, 466 U.S. at 657.

39. "About 752,000 persons, representing 91% of those sentenced for a felony in 1990 pleaded guilty. The rest were found guilty by a jury or by a judge in a bench trial." Langan & Dawson, U.S. DEP'T OF JUST., FELONY SENTENCES IN STATE COURTS, 1990, (1993).

40. Reference to the early crime surveys published in the years following the First World War may suggest that the percentage of cases disposed of by pleas of guilty has increased in subsequent years. Thus the cases canvassed in Missouri showed guilty pleas to the original charge or to lesser offenses in about 80% of the sample. MISSOURI ASSN FOR CRIM. JUST., THE MISSOURI CRIME SURVEY 315 (1926, 1968). Considerably smaller percentages of guilty

pleas are reported in Cleveland Found. Survey of Crim. Just., Criminal Justice in Cleveland 311 (1922, 1968), and *in* Illinois Assn for Crim. Just., The Illinois Crime Survey 48–49 (1929, 1968).

41. On the enlargement of prosecutorial discretion brought about by the federal sentencing guidelines, see Frankel, *Sentencing Guidelines: A Need for Creative Collaboration,* 101 Yale L.J. 2043, 2046 (1992).

42. Bordenkircher v. Hayes, 434 U.S. 357 (1978); *see* 2 W. LaFave & J. Israel, Criminal Procedure § 20.1 (1984).

43. *Cf.* 3 A.B.A., *Pleas of Guilty in* Standards for Criminal Justice 14.4–.5 (1979).

44. *E.g.,* Zimring, Eigen & O'Malley, *Punishing Homicide in Philadelphia,* 43 U. Chi. L. Rev. 227 (1976).

45. *Cf.* Schulhofer, *Is Plea Bargaining Inevitable?,* 97 Harv. L. Rev. 1037 (1984).

46. These matters are discussed in greater detail in *infra* chapter 3.

47. F. Zimring & G. Hawkins, Prison Population and Criminal Justice 13 (1992).

48. Sourcebook—1992, *supra* note 15, at 608 table 6.58; *see* Highlights, *supra* note 11, at 7 ("From 1973 to 1991, the level of crime overall declined from its peak rate in 1981. The violent crime rate has also declined in 1981.").

49. Wisotsky, *supra* note 26, at 27. For a local reaction to the Florida practices, see Editorial, *The 1,000 Foot Rule,* Gainesville Sun (Fla.), Feb. 25, 1993, at A10.

50. The discrepancies between social policy and social reality have long been a theme of public-policy scholarship. *See* E. Brodkin, *Teen Pregnancy and the Dilemmas of Social Policymaking, in* Parenthood, *supra* note 16, at 163, and the materials cited therein.

51. President Lyndon Johnson in the mid-1960s used the phrase in response to partisan criticism of his alleged neglect of the crime issue. Vorenberg, *Narrowing Discretion of Criminal Justice Officials,* 1976 Duke L.J. 651, 656. Thirty years before, Max Radin had published an incisive criticism of the war theory of criminal justice. *Enemies of Society,* J. Crim. L. & Criminology 801 (1937). No doubt, the phrase was employed much earlier.

52. In Nazi Germany, resort to the military motif was frequent. J. Jones, The Nazi Conception of Law 29 (1939) ("If the aim of the criminal law, say the Nazis, is to protect the community against anyone who threatens to break the peace, which, so they assume, is the same as threatening the existence and power of the State,

there is no reason for treating the criminal different from a foreign foe."); *see also* I. MÜLLER, HITLER'S JUSTICE 29, 76 (D. Schneider trans.) (1991).

53. E.E. Schattschneider has defined politics as "the mobilization of bias." THE SEMI-SOVEREIGN PEOPLE (1960), *quoted in* Brodkin, *supra* note 50, at 164.

54. United States v. Salerno, 481 U.S. 739, 767 (1987); *see* Baum, *supra* note 16, at 73.

55. BUREAU OF JUST. STATS., U.S. DEP'T OF JUST., DRUGS, CRIME, AND THE JUSTICE SYSTEM, NCJ 133652, at 143 (Dec. 1992) [hereinafter DRUGS, CRIME]. In late 1993 the mayor of Washington, D.C., forwarded an unsuccessful plea to President Bill Clinton for National Guard troops to assist in policing the city. *D.C. Mayor Asks for National Guard Troops,* ANN ARBOR NEWS (Mich.), Oct. 23, 1993, A1, A13.

56. *See* 18 U.S.C. § 1385 (1959); DRUGS, CRIME, *supra* note 55, at 143.

57. Baum, *supra* note 16, at 70.

58. *$2 Billion in U.S. Aid Fails To Stem Drug Flow,* GAINES-VILLE SUN (Fla.), Nov. 21, 1993, at A15.

59. Doppelt, *The Trial of the Century That Wasn't,* 78 A.B.A. J. 56 (1993). It has been alleged that an intelligence unit established with CIA assistance for the Haitian government and intended to combat the cocaine trade was used internally "as an instrument of terror." "Having created the Haitian intelligence service, the agency failed to insure that several million dollars spent training and equipping the service from 1986 to 1991 was actually used in the war on drugs." *Unit Tied to Drugs,* GAINESVILLE SUN (Fla.), Nov. 14, 1993, at A1.

60. *Cf. Drug Raids Can Invade on the Innocent,* GAINESVILLE SUN (Fla.), Sept. 26, 1993, at G1: "'It happens every day in this business,' said Capt. Art Binder of Columbia County (N.C.) Sheriff's Department, whose own officers recently raided two wrong houses before hitting, on their third try, the right one. Last year alone, police killed at least three innocent people during errant drug searches, wounded another and traumatized countless more."

61. Whether or to what degree drug-law enforcement can be said to be racially biased is, of course, much disputed. It is reported that in 1991, drug arrests for 100,000 of black population numbered 1,609. The corresponding figure for the white population was 408. It is believed that actual drug use in the two communities reveals no corresponding discrepancies. *Is the Drug War Racist?,* USA TODAY, July 23–25, 1993, at A1. Obviously more refined in-

quiry and analysis are required to establish the fact of discriminatory enforcement. *See also* H. PACKER, THE LIMITS OF THE CRIMINAL SANCTION 332–33 (1968).

62. "But the analogy of war—war against crime—is not lightly to be invoked for the general ordering of our affairs." H.L.A. HART, ESSAYS ON BENTHAM 38–39 (1982).

63. "Increasingly it is being said that fear of crime in Britain is becoming as great a problem as crime itself. Criminologists suggest that preoccupation with crime is out of all proportion to the risks; that fear is needlessly reducing the quality of people's lives; and that fear of crime can itself lead to crime—by turning cities at night into empty, forbidding places." Haugh & Mayhew, *The British Crime Survey: First Report, in* HOME OFFICE AND PLANNING UNIT REPORT 22 (1983). A somber picture of the current state of criminal justice in Britain has emerged from recent newspaper accounts. *See, e.g., Critics Say Legal Rights Latest Ulster Casualty,* CHI. TRIB., Oct. 17, 1993, § 1, at 1, 14, 15. *Cops, Courts Stifle Britons' Rights, id.,* Oct. 18, 1993, § 1, at 1, 13.

64. Zaltzman & Lederman, *The Gradual Erosion of Defendants' Status in Israeli Law,* 66 TEMP. L.Q. 1175, 1177 (1989); *see also* T. FRIEDMAN, FROM BEIRUT TO JERUSALEM 354 (1989–1990).

65. Walsh, *The Impact of Antisubversive Laws on Police Powers and Practices in Ireland: The Silent Erosion of Individual Freedom,* 62 TEMP. L.Q. 1122, 1129 (1989).

66. Sir Leon Radzinowicz lists 16 attributes of what he describes as the "authoritarian model" of criminal justice. *Supra* note 3, at 425–27. He makes clear that "to conclude . . . that the American ways of enforcing the criminal law belong to the authoritarian ways of enforcing the criminal law would be grossly misguided and unfair." *Id.* at 431. Nevertheless, at least half the attributes listed are reflected in differing degrees of intensity in current American practice.

67. Voltaire, *Commentary, in* BECCARIA, AN ESSAY ON CRIMES AND PUNISHMENTS (1953) 163 (2d Am. ed. 1819).

68. "Harmful consequences to the users or the community may be one reason that drugs are outlawed, but a direct attack on the harmful outcomes associated with drugs is beyond the pale of current federal policy. The preservation of life and the maintenance of health are explicit goals of that policy only to the extent that bad outcomes like . . . overdose deaths can be avoided by cutting the supply of drugs or the number of people who wish to take them." F. ZIMRING & G. HAWKINS, THE SEARCH FOR RATIONAL DRUG CONTROL 178 (1992); *see also* OFFICE OF NAT'L DRUG

CONTROL POL'Y, NATIONAL DRUG CONTROL 6 (1989) "Indeed, the suggestion that [there should be] a 'shift of emphasis away from drug enforcement and toward instead treatment for addicts' and the 'money saved in reduced law enforcement could be more effectively spent on health care for addicts and on preventive instruction of the rest of us' is mentioned only to be peremptorily dismissed . . . ." Honorable Jack B. Weinstein was quoted as follows: "[I]n my judicial district, the Federal probation service has had to radically cut out its drug-testing and medical treatment programs; many parents have no place to send their children for help, and, too frequently, ghetto youths seek to emulate sellers and brazenly walk city streets." *Drugs, Crime, and Punishment: The War on Drugs Is Self-Defeating,* N.Y. TIMES, July 8, 1993, at A19.

69. *See* Wisotsky, *supra* note 26, at 25–26. "[A] Harvard University survey found that almost half of the 1,035 oncologists said that they would prescribe marijuana if it were legal." *Id.* at 25; *see also* ZIMRING & HAWKINS, *supra* note 68, at 17.

70. *See* official statements collected in ZIMRING & HAWKINS, *supra* note 68, at 7–8.

71. Pub. L. No. 100-690, title V, § 5251(b), 102 Stat. 4309 (1988).

72. *Drug War Claiming Entire Generation of Young Blacks,* USA TODAY, July 27, 1993, at A7 (quoting John Laux of Minneapolis).

73. The difficulties are stated with commendable candor in an official publication. DRUGS, CRIME, *supra* note 55, at 44: "The U.S. has 88,633 miles of coastline and more than 7,500 miles of borders with Canada and Mexico. There are 300 ports of entry to the U.S. In fiscal 1991 more than 438 million people entered or re-entered the country. That year more than 128 million vehicles, 157,000 vessels, 586,000 aircraft, and 3.5 million containers also entered the U.S." Similar observations detailing the problems of interdiction during the Prohibition era abound in the reports of the Wickersham Commission, appointed by President Herbert Hoover. *See* letter to the President from George W. Wickersham, Chairman (Nov. 21, 1929), NATIONAL COMM'N ON LAW OBSERVANCE & ENFORCEMENT, PRELIMINARY REPORT ON PROHIBITION, No. 1, at 6 (1931, 1968).

74. *Four Federal Agents Are Charged in Sting,* MIAMI HERALD, Jan. 28, 1993, at 18: "Four federal agents were snared in a U.S. Customs sting aimed at uncovering dirty lawmen who allegedly ripped off drug dealers and laundered the money . . . . One F.B.I. and three Customs agents—believed to be the largest number of federal agents arrested in a single action—were charged with stealing and laundering $200,000, said Leonard Friedman, regional internal affairs director for Customs."

75. *See* Armao & Cornfeld, *Why Good Cops Turn Rotten,* N.Y. Times, Nov. 1, 1993, at A19; *Corruption Cases Involving Police Supervisors To Be Reopened,* N.Y. Times, Oct. 6, 1993 at B1, 4. Editorial, *Rogue Cops,* N.Y. Times, Oct. 1, 1993, at A14.

76. Frank Loesch, a member of the Wickersham Commission, stated in 1931: "A strong reason, among others, why I favor immediate steps being taken to revise the [Eighteenth] Amendment is in order to destroy the power of the murderous, criminal organizations flourishing all over the country upon enormous profits made in bootleg liquor traffic. These profits are the main source of the corruption funds which cement the alliance between crime and politics and corrupt the law-enforcing agencies in every populous city." NAT'L COMM'N ON LAW OBSERVANCE & ENFORCEMENT, ENFORCEMENT OF THE PROHIBITION LAWS OF THE UNITED STATES, No. 2, at 149 (1931, 1968).

77. "In addition to placing law enforcement officers under cover, long-term operations also rely on the development of informants, often low-level dealers who exchange information for leniency. The FBI has more than 3,500 informants on drug matters including over 1,700 who report exclusively on drug trafficking. These operations also depend on surveillance often including wiretaps, the analysis of financial records, telephone taps, and other activities. In 1989, 62% of the 763 State and Federal court orders for interception of wire, oral, or electronic communications resulted from investigations where narcotics violation was the most serious offense." DRUGS, CRIME, *supra* note 55, at 148–49; *see also* Wisotsky, *supra* note 26, at 16.

78. W. LaFave, Arrest 133–34 (1965); *see* N.Y. Penal Law § 35.05(1) (McKinney 1968) ("Conduct which would otherwise constitute an offense is justifiable and not criminal when . . . performed by a public servant in the reasonable exercise of his official powers, duties or functions."); UTAH CODE ANN. § 76-2-401(2) (1973).

79. The perception was expressed by Beccaria: "To prevent one crime he gives birth to a thousand. Such are the expedients of weak nations, whose laws are like temporary repairs to a tottering fabric." AN ESSAY ON CRIMES AND PUNISHMENTS, *supra* note 67, at 137; *see also* Donnelly, *Judicial Control of Informants, Spies, Stool Pigeons, and Agent Provocateurs,* 60 YALE L.J. 1091, 1093–94 (1951).

80. *E.g.,* United States v. White, 401 U.S. 745 (1971); Hoffa v. United States, 385 U.S. 293 (1966); *see* Kitch, Katz v. United States: *The Limits of the Fourth Amendment,* 1968 SUP. CT. REV. 133.

81. Junker, *The Structure of the Fourth Amendment: The*

Scope of the Protection, 79 J. Crim. Law & Criminology 1105 (1989).

82. United States v. Alvarez-Machain, 112 S. Ct. 2188 (1992).

83. *Cf.* Amsterdam, *Perspectives on the Fourth Amendment,* 58 Minn. L. Rev. 349, 377 *et seq.* (1974).

84. Skinner v. Railway Labor Executive Ass'n, 489 U.S. 602, 641 (1989); *see also* California v. Acevedo, 111 S. Ct. 1982, 2002 (1991) (Stevens, J., dissenting); United States v. Solivan, 937 F.2d 1146, 1153 (9th Cir. 1991).

85. *Cf.* Walsh, *supra* note 65, at 1102: "The purpose of this essay is to suggest that over the past two decades the Offences Against the State legislation has spearheaded a progressive, but silent, shift in the balance of the Irish criminal process. What has been viewed as exceptional is increasingly becoming accepted as the norm . . . ."

86. C. Hibert, The Roots of Evil 42–50 (1963).

87. *Quoted in* D. Thomas, Henry Fielding 310 (1990). On the "Doctrine of Maximum Severity," see 1 L. Radzinowicz, History of the English Criminal Law and Its Administration From 1750, at 321 *et seq.* (1948).

88. The number of offenses punishable by death in England at the end of the eighteenth century has been variously estimated. William Blackstone in the 1760s set the number at 160. 4 Commentaries on the Laws of England 18 (1796, 1979). It is generally assumed to have reached well over 200 in the opening decades of the next century. One remarkable statute, the Waltham Black Act, 9 Geo. 1, C. 22 (1722), by one mode of calculation, is said to have created as many as 350 capital offenses. Radzinowicz, *supra* note 87, at 3–4, 76–77.

89. In some early state constitutions in the United States the proportionality principle was expressly mandated. N.H. Const. of 1783, Bill of Rights § 18; Ohio Const. of 1802, Bill of Rights § 14. The postwar constitution of Japan also articulates the principle. *See* Dando, *Basic Concepts in and Temporal and Territorial Limits on the Applicability of Penal Law in Japan,* 9 N.Y.L. Sch. J. Int'l & Comp. L. 237, 240–43 (1988) (commentary on article 31).

90. It has long been recognized in Supreme Court adjudication that the constitutional prohibition against "cruel and unusual" punishment encompasses more than instances of barbaric methods of punishment but includes also those in which the penalties inflicted are grossly disproportionate to the culpability of the offender. Solem v. Helm, 463 U.S. 277 (1983); Robinson v. California, 370 U.S. 660, 667 (1962); Weems v. United States, 217 U.S. 349 (1910); *see* Comment, *The Eighth Amendment, Beccaria, and*

the Enlightment, 24 Buff. L. Rev. 783 (1973). In Harmelin v. Michigan, 111 S. Ct. 2680, 2684 (1991), Justice Antonin Scalia in an opinion joined by Chief Justice William Rehnquist, however, argued that the Eighth Amendment incorporates no proportionality requirement. In that case a majority of the Court upheld the constitutional validity of a Michigan statute inflicting life imprisonment without the possibility of parole for possession of 650 grams or more of a mixture containing cocaine, refusing to apply the proportionality principle in a case of a legislatively mandated penalty. The same state penalty provision was subsequently invalidated in the Supreme Court of Michigan on the authority of the "cruel or unusual" provision of the state constitution. People v. Bullock, 440 Mich. 15, 485 N.W. 2d 866 (1992).

91. *See generally* F. Zimring & G. Hawkins, Deterrence (1971); M. Mackenzie, Plato on Punishment 40–41 (1981).

92. F. Allen, Decline of the Rehabilitative Ideal: Penal Policy and Social Purpose *passim* (1981).

93. Some judges have seen social dangers in ordinary drug offenses equal to or greater than those produced by acts of violence. Harmelin v. Michigan, 111 S. Ct. 2680, 2706 (1991) (Kennedy, J. concurring); State v. Mallery, 364 So. 2d 1283, 1285 (La. 1978). While there is no ground to question the sincerity of such statements, many appear rather to reflect the prevailing zeitgeist than sober efforts at proportionality analysis.

94. *See* discussion in *infra* chapter 3.

95. See the congressional "findings" in Pub. L. no. 100–690, title V, § 5231(a), 102 Stat. 4309 (1988).

96. "In recent years, Congress has established, mainly for drug-related crimes, numerous sentences with minimum terms much longer than would otherwise be imposed under the [federal sentencing] guidelines and much longer than appear reasonable to many observers . . . . Our point is not to debate whether the criminal law should punish these offenses. That is a decision of substantive legislative policy. Rather, our concern is that the recent mandatory minimums create penalties so distorted as to hamper federal criminal adjudication. They control discretion in a way that is far more rigid than—indeed, inconsistent with—the sentencing approach Congress adopted in the 1984 Sentencing Reform Act." Report of the Federal Courts Study Committee (Hon. Joseph F. Weis, Jr., Chairman), at 133–134 (Apr. 2, 1990); *see also* Wisotsky, *supra* note 26, at 20, 34 n.40; *supra* note 49 and accompanying text.

97. "The crimes for which federal statutes currently authorize forfeiture include narcotics violations, money laundering, gam-

bling, obscenity; savings and loans offenses; and, by incorporation through RICO and money laundering statutes, a wide range of Title 18 offenses." Zeldin & Weiner, *Innocent Third Parties and Their Rights in Forfeiture Proceedings,* 28 AM. CRIM. L. REV. 843, 843 (1991); *see also Criminal Forfeiture under the Comprehensive Forfeiture Act of 1984: Raising the Stakes,* 22 AM. CRIM . L. REV. 447 (1985). The states, also, have made wide use of the forfeiture device in recent years. DRUGS, CRIME, *supra* note 55, at 186.

98. *See* Zeldin & Weiner, *supra* note 97. The Supreme Court has shown increasing concern with the procedures of forfeiture. United States v. James Daniel Good Real Property, 114 S. Ct. 492 (1993); United States v. A Parcel of Land, 113 S. Ct. 1126 (1993) ("innocent owners" and "the relation-back doctrine"). The literature is replete with instances of alleged governmental abuse in the administration of forfeiture. *E.g., Seizure of Assets in Drug Cases Raises Eyebrows,* N.Y. TIMES, Aug. 2, 1992, at A18: *Opposition Growing to Drug Forfeiture Laws* GAINESVILLE SUN (Fla.), Feb. 28, 1993, at G1; Wisotsky, *supra* note 26, at 22–23. One significant inducement to abuse may be the large financial gains enjoyed by federal, state, and local governments through asset seizure. *Seized Drug Cash Pays for Children's Play Sites,* N.Y. TIMES, July 18, 1993, at A34. In the 1980s Congress created the Assets Forfeiture Fund to receive the net profits obtained by forfeitures. 28 U.S.C. § 524 (1991). The amounts held in the Fund increased from $94 million in 1986 to $460 million in 1990. The importance of the Fund as a determinant of federal law enforcement policy is suggested in a footnote in *James Daniel Good Real Property,* 114 S. Ct. at 502 n.2: "The extent of the Government's financial stake in drug forfeiture is apparent from a 1990 memo, in which the Attorney General urged United States Attorneys to increase the volume of forfeitures in order to meet the Department of Justice's annual budget target: 'We must significantly increase production to reach our budget target . . . . Failure to achieve the $470 Million projection would expose the Department's forfeiture program to criticism and undermine confidence in our budget projections. Every effort must be made to increase forfeiture income during the remaining three months of [fiscal year] 1990.' Executive Office for United States Attorneys, U.S. Dept. of Justice, 38 United States Attorney's Bulletin 180 (1990).

99. *See supra* note 12 and accompanying text in chapter 1.

100. BECCARIA, *supra* note 67, ch. II, *"Of the Right To Punish,"* ch. VI, *"Of the Proportion Between Crimes and Punishments."* The idea of penal proportion, of course, was not an invention of the eighteenth-century Enlightenment. *See* Magna Carta (20) (1215):

"For a trivial offence, a free man shall be fined only in proportion to the degree of his offence, and for a serious offence correspondingly, but not so heavily as to deprive him of his livelihood . . . ." L. WRIGHT, MAGNA CARTA AND THE TRADITION OF LIBERTY 55 (1976).

101. N.Y., PENAL LAW § 220.21 (McKinney 1973) penalizing possession of four ounces of narcotics by a term of 15 to 25 years' imprisonment.

102. Letter by Robert Gangi, Executive Director, Correctional Association of New York, N.Y. TIMES, July 22, 1993, at A14; *see also For No. 83-A-6607, Added Years for .35 Ounces: 20 Years After Mandating Prison Terms, Few Targeted Kingpins Fill Cells,* N.Y. TIMES, Mar. 23, 1993, at B1.

103. THE MORALITY OF LAW 39 (rev. ed.) (1969).

104. J. HALL, THEFT, LAW, AND SOCIETY 118 *et seq.* (2d. ed.) (1952); *see* Petition to House of Commons by Jurors of London, 1830: "That in the present state of the law, jurors feel extremely reluctant to convict where the penal consequences of the office excite a conscientious horror on their minds, lest the rigorous performance of their duties as jurors should make them accessory to judicial murder. Hence, in courts of Justice, a most necessary and painful struggle is occasioned by the conflict of the feelings of a just humanity with the sense of the obligations of an oath." Quoted in A. KOESTLER, REFLECTIONS ON HANGING 56 (1956); *see also* J. BENTHAM, THE THEORY OF LEGISLATION 339–40 (C. Ogden ed.) (1931).

105. The judge is reported to have stated: "This is a ridiculous law, passed in the heat of passion without any thought of its real consequences. I absolutely refuse to send to prison for twenty years a young boy who has done nothing more than sell a single marijuana cigarette to a buddy . . . ." D. NEWMAN, CONVICTION: DETERMINING GUILT OR INNOCENCE WITHOUT TRIAL 178 (1966).

106. *Drugs, Crime, and Punishment: The War on Drugs Is Self-Defeating,* N.Y. TIMES, July 8, 1993, at A19 (quoting Hon. Jack B. Weinstein); *cf.* statement of Senator Phil Gramm, *Drugs, Crime, and Punishment: Don't Let Judges Set Crooks Free,* at A19.

107. *Drugs, Crime, and Punishment: The War on Drugs Is Self-Defeating, supra* note 106.

108. *Supra* note 68, at 21.

109. Whether these indications are destined to survive the political changes brought about by the 1994 state and national elections is yet to be determined.

110. Austin v. United States, 113 S. Ct. 2801 (1993); cases cited *supra* note 98.

111. Allen, *supra* note 92, at 8.

112. Amnesty Int'l, United States of America: The Death Penalty 174 (1987).

113. Thus in Gallup polls reported in June 1991, 76% of those polled answered "yes" to the question: "Are you in favor of the death penalty for persons convicted of murder?" However, 53% selected the death penalty when asked: "What do you think should be the penalty for murder—the death penalty or life imprisonment with absolutely no possibility of parole?" Sourcebook—1991, *supra* note 21, at 211 tables 2.44 & 2.45.

114. Gross, *The Romance of Revenge: Capital Punishment in America*, 13 Stu. L., Pol. & Soc'y 71, 93–95 (1993).

115. Zimring, *Inheriting the Wind: The Supreme Court and Capital Punishment During the 1990s*, 20 Fla. St. U. L. Rev. 9 (1992); *see also* Amnesty Int'l, *supra* note 112, at 228–31 app. 12.

116. Concerning England, *see* Gross, *supra* note 114, at 89–90.

117. *See generally*, Masur, *supra* note 1; Allen, *Capital Punishment, in* 2 International Encyclopedia of the Social Sciences 290 (1968).

118. Masur, *supra* note 1, *passim.*

119. Zimring, *supra* note 115, at 8–9.

120. 428 U.S. 153 (1976).

121. Sourcebook—1992, *supra* note 15, at 673 table 6.132.

122. Between 1981 and 1991, there were no executions in the northwest, 9 in the midwest, 139 in the south, and 6 in the west. *Id.* at 679 table 6.137.

123. Gross, *supra* note 114, at 96–98. On December 31, 1993 there were 363 persons under sentence of death in California. The next highest total was in Texas where the number was 357 persons. Bureau of Just. Stats., Dept. of Just., Capital Punishment 1993 at 1 (Dec. 1994).

124. *See, e.g.,* Regina v. Dudley & Stevens, 14 Q.B.D. 273 (1884); Director of Pub. Prosecutions v. Smith [House of Lords, 1961] A.C. 290. In connection with the latter case, Sir John Barry remarked: "The House of Lords held that the Court of Criminal Appeal was mistaken, and restored the judgment of death, which was not exacted, however, in conformity with the practice that a defendant whose appeal has succeeded in the court of Criminal Appeals is not executed." *Introduction,* to N. Morris & C. Howard, Studies in Criminal Law xxi (1964).

125. "An impression of disarray is necessarily communicated when life and death issues are decided by five-to-four majorities, and when whole judicial circuits split down the middle on death penalty cases." Zimring, *supra* note 115, at 19.

126. Spaziano v. Florida, 468 U.S. 447 (1984). Three states, Florida, Alabama, and Indiana, permit the judge to disregard the jury's sentencing recommendation. AMNESTY INTL, *supra* note 112, at 24. "There have been 3.6 times as many life-to death overrides (134) in Florida since 1972 as there have been death-to-life overrides (37) . . . ." Redelet & Mello, *Death-to-Life Overrides: Saving the Resources of the Florida Supreme Court,* 20 FLA. ST. U. L. REV. 196, 213 (1992).

127. AMNESTY INT'L, *supra* note 112, at 100–07. The practice of former New York Governors Alfred E. Smith and Herbert Lehman in "commuting death sentences in cases where state appeals court's decisions were divided" finds no analogue in the modern era. *Id.* at 106 n.8.

128. R. JAMES & D. AARONSON, THE INSANITY DEFENSE: A CRITICAL ASSESSMENT OF LAW AND POLICY IN THE POST-HINKLEY ERA 22–23 (1987); Perlin, *Unpacking the Myths: The Symbolism Mythology of Insanity Defense Jurisprudence,* 40 CASE W. RES. L. REV. 599 (1989–1990).

129. *E.g.,* Baroff, *Establishing Mental Retardation in Capital Cases: A Potential Matter of Life and Death,* 29 MENTAL RETARDA- TION 342 (1991); Lewis et al., *Neuropsychiatric, Psychoeducational, and Family Characteristics of 14 Juveniles Condemned to Death in the United States,* 145 AM. J. PSYCHIATRY 584 (1988); Tabak & Lane, *The Execution of Injustice,* 32 LOY. L.A. L. REV. 59 (1989); *see* Penry v. Lynaugh, 492 U.S. 302 (1989) (upholding death penalty for moderately retarded defendant).

130. AMNESTY INT'L, *supra* note 112, at 65. "Out of the thousands of executions recorded by Amnesty International throughout the world between January 1980 and May 1986, only eight in four countries were reported to have been of people who were under 18 at the time of the crime; three in the USA, two in Pakistan, one each in Bangladesh, Barbados, and Rwanda. (There were also unconfirmed reports of executions of juveniles in Iran)." *Id.* at 74.

131. Stanford v. Kentucky and Welkins v. Missouri, 492 U.S. 361 (1989) (affirming judgments of death for defendants 16 and 17 years old at time of homicides). *See* Thompson v Oklahoma, 487 U.S. 815 (1988) (reversing death penalty imposed on 15-year-old offender).

132. Gross, *supra* note 114, at 76.

133. Burt, *Disorder in the Court: The Death Penalty and the Constitution,* 85 MICH. L. REV. 1741 (1987); Weisburg, *Deregulating Death,* 1983 SUP. CT. REV. 305.

134. 428 U.S. 280, 305 (1976).

135. Barefoot v. Estelle, 463 U.S. 880 (1983); *see also Report of*

the *"Powell Commission"*: *Ad Hoc Committee on Federal Habeas Corpus in Capital Cases*, 45 CRIM. L. REP. 3239 (1989).

136. *E.g.*,Lockhart v. McCree, 106 S. Ct. 1758 (1986); Wainright v. Witt, 469 U.S. 412 (1985); Witherspoon v. Illinois, 391 U.S. 510 (1968).

137. *E.g.*, Barclay v. Florida, 463 U.S. 939, 990 (1983).

138. *Cf.* Zimring, *supra* note 115, at 15: "The larger the perceptual distance between executions and the Court, the better for the Court's internal workings and public relations."

139. Avery v. Alabama, 308 U.S. 444 (1940); Brown v. Mississippi, 297 U.S. 278 (1936); Powell v. Alabama, 287 U.S. 45 (1932).

140. *Supra* note 112, at 189.

141. *E.g.*, Furman v. Georgia, 408 U.S. 238 (1972).

142. Langan & Dawson, *Supra* note 39, at 1; *see also* Pierce & Radelet, *The Role and Consequences of the Death Penalty in American Politics*, 18 N.Y.U. REV. L. & SOC. CHANGE 711, 714 n.11 (1990–1991).

143. F. ZIMRING & G. HAWKINS, CAPITAL PUNISHMENT AND THE AMERICAN AGENDA 90 (1986).

144. For comment on the Texas statute, the constitutional validity of which was upheld in Texas v. Jurak, 428 U.S. 262 (1976), *see* Burt, *supra* note 133, at 1776–77.

145. *See, e.g.*, instances collected in Allen, *supra* note 31, at 321–22.

146. It is estimated that the expenses leading up to the 1994 conviction of the serial killer Danny Rolling in Florida exceeded $6 million. The figure does not include appeals and other postconviction costs. GAINESVILLE SUN (Fla.), Feb. 12, 1994), at A1. The average cost of executing an offender in the same state has been put at $3.2 million, a sum far exceeding that for lifetime incarceration. Radelet, *id.* (May 13, 1994), A11. "A 1982 study in New York concluded that the average capital trial and first stage of appeals would cost the tax-payer about $1.8 million, more than twice as much as it cost to keep a person in prison for life." AMNESTY INT'L, *supra* note 112, at 170.

147. "A study of criminal homicides in Georgia found, for example, that just 26 or 16 percent, of Georgia's 169 counties were responsible for 85 percent of death sentences imposed in the state from 1973 to 1978. It also found that for both felony and non-felony murder, death sentences were six times more likely to be imposed in the more rural central regions of Georgia than in the north, and seven to eight times more likely than in Fulton County in the north (which includes Atlanta, the state's capital and largest city)." AMNESTY INT'L, *supra* note 112, at 49–50; *see also supra note* 122;

Lewin, *Who Decides Who Will Die? Even Within States It Varies*, N.Y. TIMES, Feb. 23, 1995, at A1, B1.

148. Hengstler, *Attorneys for the Damned*, 73 A.B.A. J. 56 (1987); Lardent & Cohen, *The Last Best Hope: Representing Death Row Inmates*, 23 LOY. L.A. L. REV. 213 (1989); *A Shortage of Lawyers To Help the Condemned*, N.Y. TIMES, June 4, 1993, at B11.

149. 428 U.S. 153, 225 (1976).

150. 481 U.S. 279 (1987); *see also* Lockhart v. McCree, 476 U.S. 171, 173 (1986), in which evidence that "death-qualified" jury panels created under state laws are more prone to decide against the accused on the issue of guilt is regarded as irrelevant to the constitutional validity of such laws. *Cf. Amicus Brief for the American Psychological Association in* Lockhart v. McCree, AM. PSYCHOLOGIST 59, 68 (Jan. 1987): "The data demonstrating that death-qualified juries are less than neutral with respect to guilt, unrepresentative, and ineffective as compared to normal juries are now neither tentative nor fragmentary. The terms used in the relevant studies have been precisely defined. The techniques employed have been carefully articulated. The stability and convergence of the findings over three decades lend impressive support to their validity. The studies of the past decade, particularly, have closely approximated the real-life setting of the courtroom. Insofar as the social science data are relevant to the resolution of the constitutional issues at stake in this case, therefore, *amicus* believes they support affirmance of the decisions below." The skepticism of social-science data often expressed by the Court has not deterred some of its members, on occasion, from attacking opposing positions on the ground that they are unsupported by adequate scientific evidence. Thus Justice Byran White in his dissent in Miranda v. Arizona, 384 U.S. 436, 553 (1966) complained that the majority's premises concerning police interrogation were insufficient if "judged by the standards for empirical investigation utilized in the social sciences."

151. 428 U.S. at 225–26. Note the comment of Professor Burt: "From White's reasoning in *Gregg* . . . it was a short step to conclude that any judicial inquiry leading to this result must be conclusively, irrebuttably rejected. This is the position that a majority of the justices have now embraced." *Supra* note 133, at 1794–95.

152. 4 THE WORKS OF JEREMY BENTHAM 448 (J. Bowring ed.) (1962).

Chapter 3. The Structural Impediments to Legality

1. "The whole response to crime-control tends to become more crude and more cynical, displaying an increasing disregard for those fundamental considerations of a political, social and moral nature from which the foundations and the operations of the machinery of justice in a democratic society should never be cut off." Radzinowicz, *Penal Regressions,* 50 CAMBRIDGE L.J. 422, 431–32 (1991).

2. An instance of such public pressure was related by Attorney General A. Mitchell Palmer in defense of the notorious "Palmer Raids" in 1919: "I say that I was shouted at from every editorial sanctum in America from sea to sea; I was preached at from every pulpit; I was urged—I could feel it dinned into my ears—throughout the country to do something and do it now, and do it quick, and do it in a way that should bring results to stop this thing in the United States." *Quoted in* F. ALLEN, THE CRIMES OF POLITICS 55 (1974).

3. *See, e.g.,* THE ROYAL NORWEGIAN MINISTRY OF JUST., ADMINISTRATION OF JUSTICE IN NORWAY (1957); R. JACKSON, THE MACHINERY OF JUSTICE IN ENGLAND *passim* (4th ed.) (1964).

4. The condition of decentralization has been widely noted for several decades. *E.g.,* R. CALDWELL, CRIMINOLOGY 309 (2d ed. 1965); Note, *Disorganization of Metropolitan Law Enforcement and Some Proposed Solutions,* J. CRIM. L. & CRIMINOLOGY 63 (1952). "In fact, our whole scheme of police organization is largely based on the concept of local autonomy. Decentralization and fragmentation 'are among the most striking characteristics of American police patterns, since no other part of the world has carried local autonomy to such extreme lengths.'" W.R. LaFAVE, ARREST 128 (1965) (quoting B. SMITH, POLICE SYSTEMS IN THE UNITED STATES 342 (1940)).

5. See discussion *infra,* chapter 3.

6. George, *The Japanese Judicial System: Thirty Years of Transition,* 12 LOY. L.A. L. REV. 807, 830 (1979).

7. Measures taken in Michigan to achieve a greater coordination of the judicial function illustrate the modern tendency. *See* Judges v. Wayne County, 386 Mich. 1, 190 N.W.2d 228 (1972), *cert. denied,* 405 U.S. 923 (1972).

8. Demonstration of the validity of the insight is one of the important contributions of the American Bar Foundation's *Survey of the Administration of Criminal Justice in the United States,* conducted in the mid-1950s. The insight is expressed in a series of

volumes engendered by the *Survey's* Pilot Studies. *E.g.*, D. NEW-
MAN, CONVICTION: DETERMINING GUILT OR INNOCENCE WITHOUT
TRIAL (1966); LaFAVE, *supra* note 4.

9. The phrase is that of Heinz and Manikas in their *Networks
Among Elites in a Local Criminal Justice System,* 26 LAW & SOC.
REV. 831, 832 (1992) (citing Hagan, *Why Is There So Little Criminal
Justice Theory? Neglected Macro- and Micro-Level Links Between
Organization and Power,* 26 J. RES. IN CRIME & DELINQ. 116, 119
(1989)).

10. *Id.* at 850: "But if the present, unsettled state of Chicago
politics is typical of that in most major American cities, as we
suspect that it is, then we would expect to find that the structure of
communication among criminal justice elites in other cities is also
balkanized."

11. A federal study published in the early 1990s showed that
most state and local agencies with primary narcotic drug responsibility participated in multijurisdictional task forces. "More than
three-quarters of the local police and sheriff's agencies that serve
populations of 100,000 or more participated in such task forces."
BUREAU OF JUST. STATS., U.S. DEP'T OF JUST., DRUGS, CRIME,
AND THE JUSTICE SYSTEM NCJ-133652, at 142–43 (Dec. 1992).

12. *E.g., Sheriff Doesn't Want to Join Drug Task Force,* GAINES-
VILLE SUN (Fla.), June 22, 1993, at A1, A6.

13. *Poor Cooperation Deflates F.B.I. Report on Hate Crime,* N.Y.
TIMES, Jan. 6, 1993, at A8.

14. In 1977 the Comptroller General submitted a report to
Congress on the subject of such task forces. The conclusions of the
report are made apparent by its title, *War on Organized Crime Is
Faltering—Federal Strike Forces Not Getting the Job Done* (Report
to the Congress by the Comptroller General of the United States
GGD-77-17, 1977).

15. K. DAVIS, POLICE DISCRETION 37–38, 48–50 (1975). Some
15 years later, a "Coordinating Council" including officials from
various agencies and formed to deal with problems of overcrowding in the Cook County jail is reported not to have evolved into an
effective agency for coordination of policy efforts other than those
relating to jail overcrowding, and "indeed, there is much reason to
doubt about whether it has taken productive action concerning
even these issues." Heinz & Manicas, *supra* note 9, at 850.

16. *Cf.* "[A]nother general rationale for some level of formality
has to do with who is to decide, not the content of what is decided."
Summers, *Theory, Formality, and Practical Legal Criticism,* 106
LAW Q. REV. 407, 420 (1990).

17. F. ZIMRING & G. HAWKINS, THE SEARCH FOR RATIONAL DRUG CONTROL 165 (1992).

18. F. ZIMRING & G. HAWKINS, PRISON POPULATION AND CRIMINAL POLICY IN CALIFORNIA 66, 67 (1992).

19. *See* discussion in *supra* chapter 2.

20. T.M. COOLEY, CONSTITUTIONAL LIMITATIONS 189 (2d ed.) (1871); *see also* People v. Hurlbut, 24 Mich. 44 (1871).

21. It should be noted, however, that some members of Congress espousing decentralization of governmental authority in many areas of public policy have, nevertheless, supported the increasing federalization of criminal law and other interventions in local law enforcement areas hitherto assumed to be the exclusive province of the states. *See supra* note 24 in chapter 2.

22. The variety of tasks imposed on police departments, large and small, is formidable and not generally appreciated. Much of what the police are called upon to do has little or nothing to do with criminal law enforcement but involves such functions as traffic control, first aid and ambulance assistance, and an aggregation of what are essentially social welfare services.

23. HALE, PLEAS OF THE CROWN ch. XI (1736); Pearson, *The Right To Kill in Making Arrests,* 28 MICH. L. REV. 957 (1930).

24. Tennessee v. Garner, 471 U.S. 1, 18–19 (1985); *see also* C. MILTON, J. HALLECK & G. ABRECHT, POLICE USE OF DEADLY FORCE 45–46 (1977).

25. Comment, *Criminal Justice in Extremis: Administration of Justice During the April 1968 Chicago Disorder,* 36 U. CHI. L. REV. 455 (1969); M. JANOWITZ, SOCIAL CONTROL OF ESCALATED RIOTS (1968); Mattick, *Form and Content of Recent Riots,* 9 MIDWAY 3 (Summer 1968); *Violence in the City—An End or a Beginning?* (Report of Governor's Commission on the Los Angeles Riots, Dec. 2, 1965).

26. Hudnut, *The Police and the Polis: A Mayor's Perspective, in* POLICE LEADERSHIP IN AMERICA 26–27 (W. Geller ed.) (1985); A. REISS, THE POLICE AND THE PUBLIC 114–15 (1971); *cf.* Vorenberg, *Narrowing the Discretion of Criminal Justice Officials,* 1976 Duke L.J. 651, 658 n.11.

27. In the early 1990s, the beating of Rodney King by members of the Los Angeles Police Department resulted in criminal trials of the officers involved in state and federal courts and a civil suit against the City of Los Angeles in which the plaintiff prevailed. In Detroit, a criminal trial of officers for the killing of a black victim in police custody resulted in convictions. *4 Detroit Officers Charged in Death,* N.Y. TIMES, Nov. 17, 1992, at A1, A11.

28. *E.g., Grand Jury Indicts 3 Newark Officers,* N.Y. TIMES, Sept. 20, 1992, at A1; *Killing by Officer Prompts Protest, id.,* Nov. 18, 1992, at A1; *FBI Reviews Tenn. Police Beating Case,* GAINESVILLE SUN (Fla.), Dec. 18, 1992, at A4. A single issue of the LAW ENFORCE-MENT NEWS, May 15, 1992, at 2–3, 4, 5, 6, 7, reported 18 incidents of alleged police misconduct drawn from the entire country. More than half of these involved the alleged use of illegal violence.

29. *E.g., Police Oppose Citizen Review Panels,* ANN ARBOR NEWS, Dec. 27, 1992, at A9.

30. Williams, *Police Rulemaking Revisited: Some New Thoughts on an Old Problem,* 47 LAW & CONTEMP. PROBS. 123 (1984).

31. Allen, *The Judicial Quest for Penal Justice: The Warren Court and the Criminal Cases,* 1975 U. ILL. L.F. 518, 523.

32. *Id.* at 525: "We have not been ingenious in devising institutions that subject criminal justice functions to scrutiny and test. This failure to devise alternative institutions charged with such responsibilities explains in part the willingness of American courts to enter these areas. The same fact helps explain the particular forms that judicial intervention has taken." *See also* Amsterdam, *The Supreme Court and the Rights of Suspects in Criminal Cases,* 45 N.Y.U. L. REV. 785, 790 (1970).

33. Terry v. Ohio, 392 U.S. 1 (1968).

34. DAVIS, *supra* note 15, at 127.

35. Junker, *The Structure of the Fourth Amendment: The Scope of the Protection,* 79 J. CRIM. L. & CRIMINOLOGY 1105 (1989).

36. The point is usefully examined in LaFave, *Controlling Discretion by Administrative Regulations: The Use, Misuse, and Nonuse of Police Rules and Policies in Fourth Amendment Adjudication,* 89 MICH. L. REV. 442 (1990).

37. Allen, *Commentary,* 39 U. FLA. L. REV. 545 (1987).

38. Police discretion has been the object of considerable investigation in the generation just past, much of it prompted in the first instance by the American Bar Foundation's *Survey of the Administration of Criminal Justice in the United States, supra* note 8. *See, e.g.,* Center, *Police Discretion: A Selected Bibliography,* 47 LAW & CONTEMP. PROBS. 303 (1984). A pioneering study of the issues making extensive use, inter alia, of the *Survey's* Pilot Studies and one retaining much modern relevance is W. LAFAVE, ARREST (1965).

39. It should be noted that such decisions have broad systemic significance. Decisions made by the police not to invoke the criminal process are generally made to preserve police resources, not those of other parts of the system. The absence of visible guide-

lines not only creates the danger of capricious and arbitrary reactions at the police level but may also destroy the opportunity to guide police discretion toward more effective fulfillment of broader, system-wide goals. *See* LaFave, *supra* note 38, at 103–04.

40. Much vagrancy legislation, in practice, delegates to the police a power to define the actual standards for its application in the situations encountered on patrol.

41. Legislatures have often found it difficult to draft gambling legislation immunizing casual social gamblers without seriously weakening its effectiveness against professional gamblers and their patrons. Typically, such legislation is stated overbroadly, reliance being placed on the police and prosecutors to withhold application from social gamblers. *See* A.B.A., COMMENTARY ON THE MODEL ANTIGAMBLING ACT (1952), *quoted in* LaFave, *supra* note 38, at 89.

42. F. ALLEN, THE BORDERLAND OF CRIMINAL JUSTICE: ESSAYS IN LAW AND CRIMINOLOGY 7–9 (1964).

43. Breitel, *Controls in Criminal Law Enforcement,* 27 U. CHI. L. REV. 427, 427 (1960).

44. "[D]iscretion—even legally permissible discretion—involves great hazard. It makes easy the arbitrary, the discriminatory, and the oppressive. It produces inequality of treatment. It offers a fertile bed for corruption. It is conducive to the development of the police state—or, at least, a police-minded state." *Id.* at 429.

45. *Cf.* Skolnick, *Operational Environment and Police Discretion, in* JUSTICE WITHOUT TRIAL (J. Skolnick ed.) (1966); Wilson, *Police Discretion, in* VARIETIES OF POLICE BEHAVIOR (1968).

46. *Cf.* LaFave, *supra* note 38, at 114: "The obvious dilemma is that the Negro continues to be judged by a different standard because it is assumed that he has a greater tolerance for certain kinds of antisocial conduct, and existing differences in attitude are probably reinforced by the fact that different standards are applied by enforcement agencies."

47. Professor LaFave quotes the language of the Milwaukee Police Department's Rules and Regulations, rule 29 sec. 3 (1950): The police "shall at all times within the boundaries of the City, preserve the public peace, prevent crime, detect and arrest violators of the law, protect life and property and enforce all the criminal laws of the State of Wisconsin and the ordinances of the City . . . ."; LaFave *supra* note 38 at 157; *see also* Williams, *supra* note 30, at 133–34.

48. Accurate and full reporting to administrative superiors by police officers and greater and more systematic scrutiny of the

filed reports by supervisors are important conditions to effective guidance of police discretion. The conditions are often inadequately fulfilled in much American police practice.

49. These matters are extensively discussed in LaFave, *supra* note 36. *See also* H. GOLDSTEIN, POLICING A FREE SOCIETY 179 (1977).

50. *E.g.,* Colorado v. Bertine, 479 U.S. 367 (1987); Illinois v. Lafayette, 462 U.S. 640 (1983); South Dakota v. Opperman, 428 U.S. 364 (1976).

51. "Beyond the improvements in internal administration there is need for, at least, state-wide centralized administrative supervision and enforcement of standards." Breitel, *supra* note 43, at 433.

52. Far-reaching proposals for rule-guided policing in the United States advanced in the 1970s have not as yet come to fruition. *E.g.,* Amsterdam, *supra* note 32. McGowan, *Rule-Making and the Police,* 70 MICH. L. REV. 659 (1972). Interest in advancing internal rule making has been strong, however, in some American police departments. GOLDSTEIN, *supra* note 49, at 117. The objective of more effective guidance and containment of police discretion continues to be an active item on the agenda of criminal justice reform.

53. Linnan, *Police Discretion in a Continental European Administrative State: The Police of Baden-Württemberg in the Federal Republic of Germany,* 47 LAW & CONTEMP. PROBS. 186, 186–87 (1984).

54. Jackson, *The Federal Prosecutor,* 24 J. AM. JUDICATURE SOC'Y 18 (1940); *see also* Vorenberg, *supra* note 26, at 678: "The prosecutor's discretion whether or what to charge is the broadest discretionary power in criminal administration." During the year ending June 30, 1990, approximately 2,400 chief prosecutors employed about 20,000 deputy attorneys for the prosecution of felony cases in the state courts. J. DAWSON, S. SMITH & C. DEFRANCIS, U.S. DEPT OF JUST., PROSECUTORS IN STATE COURTS, 1992 at 2 (Mar. 1992).

55. *Cf.* Weigend, *Prosecution: Comparative Aspects, in* 3 ENCYLOPEDIA OF CRIME & JUSTICE 1296, 1301 (1983).

56. In a survey of 63 countries conducted by the United Nations, 15 of the responding countries indicated adherence to the "legality principle" (every case must be prosecuted when there is sufficient evidence) and 13 applied the principle in most cases. TRENDS IN CRIME AND CRIMINAL JUSTICE, 1970–1985, IN THE CONTEXT OF SOCIO-ECONOMIC CHANGE (United Nations, 1992). *But see*

Weigend, supra note 55, at 1300: "Austrian law does not offer any loopholes for declining to prosecute petty cases, yet overall dismissal rates are not significantly lower than in other European countries . . . . Discretionary dismissals of minor offenses are effectively concealed behind the label of 'insufficient evidence.'"

57. Attorney General Sir Hartley Shorecross was quoted as follows: "It has never been the rule in this country—I hope it never will be—that suspected criminal offences must automatically be the subject of prosecution. Indeed, the very first . . . regulations under which the director of public prosecutions worked provided that he should . . . prosecute 'wherever the offence or the circumstances of its commission is or are of such a character that the prosecution in respect thereof is required in the public interest.' That is still the dominant consideration." Wood, *Prosecution Policy in England and Wales,* ASIAN J. CRIME PREVENTION & CRIM. JUST. 37 (Nov. 8, 1990).

58. The *"Guidelines for Crown Prosecutors"* in the Prosecution of Offences Act, 1985, 12 Halsbury Stat. (4th ed.), 1989 reissue (Eng.) states:
(1) The Director shall issue a Code for Crown Prosecutors giving guidance on general principles to be applied by them—(a) in determining, in any case—(i) whether proceedings for an offence should be instituted or, where proceedings have been instituted, whether they should be discontinued; or (ii) what charges should be preferred; and (b) in considering, in any case, representations to be made by them to any magistrates' court about the mode of trial suitable for that case." Although the provision's terms are applicable only to the director of public prosecutions and the Crown prosecuting service, the attorney general has indicated that the provisions are to be applicable to all prosecuting departments in England, Wales, and Northern Ireland. Wood, *supra* note 57, at 39–40.

59. Thus Williams, *Good Government by Prosecutorial Decree: The Use and Abuse of Mail Fraud,* 32 ARIZ. L. REV. 137, 145–46 (1990), points out that the then-current departmental *Manual* provided little guidance to prosecutors in one of the most important categories of federal prosecutions, that of mail and wire fraud. *But see* RICO prosecutorial guidelines, UNITED STATES ATTORNEYS' MANUAL §§ 9–110.100, .200, .300, .400. (rev. 1990). Budgetary controls exercised at the departmental level may, of course, significantly limit the options available to United States attorneys.

60. Insights into the sources and strength of decentralization of federal prosecutions can be gained from the debate in Toensing,

Time To Rein In U.S. Attorneys, LEGAL TIMES 24 (Jan. 11, 1993), and Obermaier, *United States Attorneys: Don't Rein 'Em In, id.,* at 37 (Feb. 8, 1993).

61. George, *supra* note 6, at 830; Weigend, *supra* note 55, at 1297; West, *Prosecution Review Commissions; Japan's Answer to the Problems of Prosecutorial Discretion,* 92 COLUM. L. REV. 684, 690–91 (1992).

62. See discussion *infra,* chapter 3.

63. These matters are discussed more fully in *supra* chapter 2.

64. The very existence of broad discretionary powers in the American prosecutor invites efforts to influence their exercise by persons and groups displaying widely differing motivations. *Cf.* Weigend, *supra* note 55, at 1300: "Many Austrian and German prosecutors welcome the absence of discretion as a shield against pressure from the outside."

65. There is considerable variation in the uses made of grand juries across the country. Recent statistics report that in 42% of state prosecutorial districts, no grand juries are employed. In fewer than half (48%) of the districts did the prosecutor appear before the grand jury. *See* U.S. DEPT. OF JUST., BUREAU OF JUST. STATS., SOURCEBOOK OF CRIMINAL JUSTICE STATISTICS—1991, at 87 table 1.89 (1992).

66. *E.g.,* Dyer v. Boles, 368 U.S. 448, 456 (1962).

67. Baker, *The Prosecutor: Initiation of Prosecution,* 23 J. CRIM. L. & CRIMINOLOGY, 770 (1933). At least some modern American judges reveal little enthusiasm for a more active judicial role. Then–Circuit Judge Warren Burger wrote: "Few subjects are less adapted to judicial review than the exercise by the Executive of his discretion when and whether to institute criminal proceedings, or what precise charges will be made, or whether to dismiss a proceeding once brought." Newman v. United States, 382 F.2d 479, 480 (D.C. Cir. 1967). More recently, the Supreme Court has denied power in the federal district courts to dismiss an otherwise valid indictment because the prosecutor had withheld exculpatory evidence from the grand jury. United States v. Williams, 112 S. Ct. 1735 (1992).

68. A.B.A., STANDARDS 73 *et seq.* (1974). A recent study, however, suggests an overall decline in the use of explicit, internally generated criteria relating to the conduct of plea bargaining: "In 1974, 80% of the chief prosecutors reported having explicit criteria and time limits on plea negotiation, but by 1990 the percentage had fallen to 36%." Dawson, *supra* note 54, at 6 table 14.

69. "States should strengthen the coordination of local prosecution by enhancing the authority of the State attorney general or

some other appropriate statewide officer and by establishing a State council of prosecutors comprising all local prosecutors under the leadership of the attorney general." PRESIDENT'S COMM'N ON LAW ENFORCEMENT & THE ADMIN. OF JUST., THE CHALLENGE OF CRIME IN A FREE SOCIETY 149 (1967); *see also* Vorenberg, *supra* note 26, at 681–682.

70. For a varied listing of authorities critical of the federal guidelines, see Freed, *Federal Sentencing in the Wake of Guidelines: Unacceptable Limits on the Discretion of Sentencers,* 101 YALE L. J. 1681, 1685–86 n.10. The literature is voluminous. *See, e.g.,* Symposium, *Punishment, id.,* at 1681 *et seq.; Symposium on Federal Sentencing Articles,* 66 S. CAL. L. REV. 99–657 (1992); Symposium, *A Decade of Sentencing Guidelines: Revisiting the Role of the Legislature,* 28 WAKE FOREST L. REV. 181–507 (1993); *Federal Sentencing Guidelines Symposium,* 29 AM. CRIM. L. REV. 771–932 (1992).

71. M. FRANKEL, CRIMINAL SENTENCES 8 (1973). "[M]y first basic point is this: the almost unchecked and sweeping powers we give to judges in the fashioning of sanctions are terrifying and intolerable for a society that professes devotion to the rule of law." *Id.* at 5.

72. MINNESOTA SENTENCING GUIDELINES AND COMMENTARY ANNOTATED (1985); *see also* Note, *Introduction to the Minnesota Sentencing Guidelines,* 5 HAMLINE L. REV. 293 (1982).

73. Authorization for the present federal system was provided in the Comprehensive Crime Control Act of 1984, Pub. L. No. 98–433, 98 Stat. 2200. *See especially* the Sentencing Reform Act of 1984, 18 U.S.C. §§ 3551–3586 (Supp. 1985).

74. Allen, *Criminal Sentencing in the United States: A Survey in Aid of Comparative Study, in* CONFLICT AND INTEGRATION IN THE WORLD TODAY 439, 444–45 (1988).

75. Disputes over the definition of disparity reflect a radical absence of consensus among judges concerning the factors relevant to sentencing and the priorities to be assigned them characterized sentencing practices in American courts. "A striking illustration emerged in a . . . conference of federal trial judges of the Second Circuit . . . . The facts from numerous cases were selected from the files, and each of the fifty judges present was asked to state what sentences he would have imposed. The results, in some instances, were striking discrepancies. In one case, a crime that drew a three-year sentence from one judge drew a twenty-year term and a $65,000 fine from another. These disparities could not be attributed to differences in the cases being decided, since each judge was deciding on the identical set of assumed facts." A. VON HIRSCH, DOING JUSTICE 29 (Report of the Committee for

the Study of Incarceration) (1976); *see also* Partridge & Eldridge, A REPORT TO THE JUDGES OF THE SECOND CIRCUIT (Fed. Judicial Center, Aug. 1974); S. WHEELER, K. MANN & A. SARAT, SITTING IN JUDGMENT: THE SENTENCING OF WHITE COLLAR CRIMINALS (1988).

76. *See* Frankel, *Sentencing Guidelines: A Need for Creative Collaboration,* 101 YALE L.J. 2043, 2047 (1992).

77. *See* discussion in *supra* chapter 2.

78. 1990 ANN. REP. OF U.S. SENTENCING COMM'N table C-4. "Congress . . . told the Commission that guidelines were 'to be formulated to minimize the likelihood that the federal prison population will exceed the capacity of the Federal prisons.' The Commission on the whole seems to have ignored that mandate. It shares with Congress the credit for overfilling the federal prisons to something like 160% of capacity." Frankel, *supra* note 76; *see* ZIMRING & HAWKINS, *supra* note 18; Alschuler, *The Failure of Sentencing Guidelines: A Plea for Less Aggregation,* 58 U. CHI. L. REV. 901, 936 (1991).

79. N. MORRIS & M. TONRY, BETWEEN PRISON AND PROBATION: INTERMEDIATE PUNISHMENTS IN A RATIONAL SENTENCING SYSTEM (1990); *see also* Baer *When Prison Isn't Enough,* 6 CRIM. JUSTICE 2 (1991): "The U.S. Sentencing Commission failed to consider seriously the recommendations for intermediate sanctions, thereby missing an opportunity to reduce costs, relieve prison overcrowding, and enhance fairness in the sentencing system that a system of intermediate sanctions might provide. Morris and Tonry were unfortunately . . . correct when they described the Sentencing Commission's approach to alternatives to incarceration and the interchangeability of punishments as 'ungenerous and unimaginative.'"

80. *E.g.,* Freed, *supra* note 70, at 1703–18.

81. Alschuler, *supra* note 78, *passim.*

82. "The sentencing reform movement has not restricted sentencing discretion so much as it has transferred discretion from judges to prosecutors." *Id.* at 926; *see also* Frankel, *supra* note 76, at 2046; Freed, *supra* note 70, at 1697. One of the factors that have tended to enhancement of prosecutorial power is the mandating of "real offense" sentencing in the federal courts. That the resulting practices have given rise to serious constitutional issues is asserted in Lear, *Is Conviction Irrelevant?,* 40 UCLA L. REV. 1179 (1993); *see also* Reitz, *Sentencing Facts: Travesties of Real-Offense Sentencing,* 45 STAN. L. REV. 523 (1993).

83. *See* Freed, *supra* note 70, at 1684: "Discretionary actors, including judges, prosecutors, defense attorneys, and probation

officers, find themselves torn between allegiance to rigid rules and an urge to do justice in individual cases." *See also* Vorenberg, *supra* note 26, at 663.

84. *See* Nagel & Schulhofer, *A Tale of Three Cities: An Empirical Study of Charging and Bargaining Practices Under the Federal Sentencing Guidelines,* 66 So. CAL. L. REV. 501, 558 (1992): "An effort to address causes rather than symptoms must confront the kinds of problems that participants experience in working with the guidelines. Principally there needs to be greater flexibility in the guidelines system. Yet an effort to achieve such flexibility must remain attuned to the need to preserve a system of structured discretion that avoids opening the sentencing process to widespread and problematic disparities like those that prompted the Sentencing Reform Act . . . . What is at stake is the subtle balance between flexibility and structure, a balance we believe may need refinement." *See also* Schulhofer, *Assessing the Federal Sentencing Process: The Problem Is Uniformity, Not Disparity,* 29 AM. CRIM. L. REV. 833 (1992).

85. The problems of reconciling the claims of individualized justice with the needs and capacities of a legal order have rarely been portrayed so effectively as in Norval Morris's "parable" *The Brothel Boy. See* his THE BROTHEL BOY AND OTHER PARABLES OF THE LAW 11–24 (1992).

86. *Cf., e.g.,* Tonry, *The Success of Judge Fraenkel's Sentencing Commission,* 64 COLO. L. REV. 713 (1993): "The experience of the federal commission is misleading . . . . [T]he federal commission is but one of a dozen or more. In some states, notably Delaware, Minnesota, Oregon, Pennsylvania, and Washington, the experience has been much happier."

87. BECCARIA, AN ESSAY ON CRIMES AND PUNISHMENTS 24 (1953) (2d Am. ed. 1819). Beccaria states further: "Every man hath his own particular point of view, and, at different times, sees the same objects in very different lights. The spirit of the laws will then be the result of the good or bad logic of the judge; and this will depend on his good or bad digestion, on the violence of his passions, on the rank or condition of the accused, and on all those little circumstances which change the appearance of objects in the fluctuating mind of man." *Id.* at 23–24.

88. *Cf.* E. LEVI, AN INTRODUCTION TO LEGAL REASONING 30–31 (1949).

89. *E.g.,* State v. Williquette, 129 Wis. 2d 239, 385 N.W.2d 145 (1986). For comment on the case, *see* Allen, *The Erosion of Legality in American Criminal Justice,* 29 ARIZ. L. REV. 385, 396–97 (1987).

90. Judge Patricia Wald's 1981 study indicated that references

to legislative history were made in virtually all cases in the United States Supreme Court involving questions of statutory interpretation. *Some Observations on the Use of Legislative History in the 1981 Supreme Court Term*, 68 Iowa L. Rev. 195 (1983). Justice Antonin Scalia has been one to protest the practices. *See* Green v. Bock Laundry Mach. Co., 490 U.S. 504, 528 (1989) (Scalia, J. concurring). The English Law Commission (No. 21) and the Scottish Law Commission (No. 11) in 1969 rejected a proposal to relax the inhibitions on the use of Parliamentary materials in judicial interpretations of statutes. The Interpretation of Statutes 36 (1969).

91. "English judges generally emphasize the overall primacy of ordinary meaning of words used in the statute far more than do most American judges." P. Atiyah & R. Summers, Form and Substance in Anglo-American Law 101 (1987); *see id.* at 100–112. It should not be supposed that contending theories of statutory interpretation are absent in England. Note the discussion of the "golden" and "mischief" rules in The Interpretation of Statutes, *supra* note 90, at 17. Statutory interpretation as practiced in English courts has on occasion inspired criticism at home and from foreign observers. *Id.* at 9; Frankfurter, *Some Reflections on the Reading of Statutes*, 47 Colum. L. Rev. 527, 540–42 (1947).

92. Summers, *A Formal Theory of the Rule of Law*, 6 Ratio Juris 127, 132–33 (1993).

93. Mr. Sammler's Planet 228 (1970).

94. Summers & Marshall, *The Argument from Ordinary Meaning in Statutory Interpretation*, 43 N. Ir. Legal Q. 215, 226 (1992). *But cf.* statement by Sen. Arlen Specter *quoted in* Brudney, *Congressional Commentary on Judicial Interpretations of Statutes*, 93 Mich. L. Rev. 1, 28 (1994): "[M]embers of Congress are more likely to read a committee report than the bill itself. The prose is easier to understand, and, because a bill usually amends an existing statute, it is impossible to follow without referring to the U.S. Code."

95. Levi, *supra* note 88, at 32.

96. Allen, *supra* note 89, at 397–400. One of the influences contributing to the waning of the rule of strict interpretation of criminal statutes is its rejection in the drafting of Model Penal Code § 1.02(3) pt. I (1985): "The provisions of the Code shall be construed according to the fair import of their terms but when the language is susceptible of differing constructions it shall be interpreted to further the general purposes stated in the Section and the special purposes of the particular provisions involved." *See*

Greenawalt, *A Vice of Its Virtues: The Perils of Precision in Criminal Codification,* 19 RUTGERS L. REV. 929, 935–36 (1988).

97. Tit. IX, § 904a, 84 Stat. 941–947 (1970). *See* Bradley, *Racketeers, Congress, and the Courts,* 65 IOWA L. REV. 837, 838 (1980) ("[T]he courts reflecting the natural fear of racketeering, have extended RICO beyond the broadest boundaries permitted by the statutory language . . . ."); *see also* Atkinson, *Racketeer Influenced Corrupt Organizations: 18 U.S.C. § 1961–68: Broadest of the Federal Criminal Statutes,* 69 J. CRIM. L. & CRIMINOLOGY 1, 3 (1978). Not all federal judges have rallied to the congressional call for broad interpretation of the RICO legislation. *See* United States v. Mandel, 415 F. Supp 997, 1022 (D. Md. 1976).

98. See discussion *infra,* chapter 3.

99. Smith v. United States, 113 S. Ct. 2050 (1993).

100. Hart, *Jurisprudence Through English Eyes: The Nightmare and the Noble Dream,* 11 GA. L. REV. 969 (1977).

101. *Cf.* THE INTERPRETATION OF STATUTES, *supra* note 90, at 13: "[I]n those countries which require courts to review the constitutionality of legislation, there is an important residual effect on the approach to interpretation even in cases not involving a constitutional issue."

102. ATIYAH & SUMMERS, *supra* note 91, at 315 *et seq.*

103. *Id.* at 316–17.

104. See discussion *infra,* chapter 3.

105. Thus, the Omnibus Crime Control & Safe Streets Act of 1968, Pub. L. no. 90–351, 82 Stat. 197 (codified as amended in scattered sections of 5, 18, 28, 40, 41, 42, 47 U.S.C.), contains 10 titles and occupies 42 pages in *Statutes at Large.* The Organized Crime Control Act of 1970, Pub. L. No. 91–452, 84 Stat. 922 (codified as amended in scattered sections of 7, 12, 15, 16, 19, 21, 28, 29, 33, 42, 45, 46, 47, 49, 50 U.S.C.), of which the RICO legislation is part, contains 10 titles and covers 39 pages. The Drug Abuse Act of 1988, Pub. L. No. 100–690, 102 Stat. 4181 (codified as amended in scattered sections of 21, 42 U.S.C.) contains 10 titles and covers 366 pages. The Violent Crime Control & Law Enforcement Act of 1994, Pub. L. No. 103–322 [H.R. 3355], 108 Stat. 1796 *et seq.,* contains 33 titles and covers 356 pages.

106. For instances of such malfunctioning, see United States v. Bass, 404 U.S. 388 (1971); United States v. Five Gambling Devices, 346 U.S. 441 (1953).

107. *Cf.* Posner, *Legal Formalism, Legal Realism, and the Interpretation of Statutes and the Constitution,* 37 CASE W. RES. L. REV. 179, 189–90 (1986).

108. The symbiotic relationship between courts and legislatures in the United States frequently results in the enhancement of the judicial role. Administration of the "void for vagueness" doctrine supplies one example. The rule posits that statutory language may descend so far into incomprehensibility that efforts to apply it constitute denials of due process of law. The doctrine has been applied sparingly, however; some may believe with excessive caution. *But cf.* Comment, *RICO's "Pattern" Requirement: Void for Vagueness?,* 90 COLUM. L. REV. 489 (1990). In denying wider application, judges often cite the necessity of judicial restraint when called on to invalidate the products of a coordinate branch of government. Yet in announcing the self-restraining ordinance, the courts are in fact expanding their lawmaking roles at the expense of the legislature. For in proceeding to assign intelligible meaning to a grossly defective statute, the courts, under the guise of interpretation, exercise a legislative authority.

109. *The American Doctrine of Constitutional Law,* 7 HARV. L. REV. 129, 155–56 (1893).

110. Larceny Act, 1861, § 23 (Eng.).

111. In Cotterill v. Penn [1936] 1 K.B. 53, the court interpreted the statute as creating a strict criminal liability.

112. *See* MODEL PENAL CODE §§ 1.04(5), 2.05 pt. I (1985). Legislative proposals designed to respond to the problem have been advanced in Great Britain. *See* Law Commission, Working Paper No. 31 (Second Programmer, Item XVIII), *Codification of the Criminal Law* 6 (Law Comm. No. 125) (1970).

113. Internal Security Act, No. 74 of 1982 (as amended by Internal Security Amendment Act, No. 66 of 1986), STAT. REP. S. AFR. (Criminal Law & Procedure), at 1291 *et seq.* [hereinafter Internal Security Act, no. 74].

114. Nagen & Albrecht, *Judicial Executions and Individual Responsibility Under International Law,* United Nations Center Against Apartheid (Apr. 1988).

115. A. MATHEWS, FREEDOM, SECURITY, AND THE RULE OF LAW 43 (1986).

116. *Id.* at 221.

117. Internal Security Act, No. 74, § 55, *supra* note 113.

118. "[A]ny doctrine, ideology or scheme . . . which is based on, has developed from or is related to the tenets of Karl Marx, Engels, Vladimer Lenin or Mao Tse-Tung, or of any other recognized theorist in connection with or exponent of those tenets, and which aim at the establishment of any form of socialism or collective ownership") *Quoted in* S. ELLMAN, IN A TIME OF TROUBLES 17 (1992).

119. Internal Security Act, No. 74, § 54(1)(b), *supra* note 113.

120. *Id.* at § 54(c).

121. First Amendment questions have arisen in RICO cases involving state pornography statutes. Fort Wayne Books v. Indiana, 489 U.S. 46 (1989); *see also* Nuger, *The RICO/CRRA Trap: Troubling Implications for Adult Expression,* 23 IND. L. REV. 109 (1990). First Amendment questions have also surfaced in connection with uses of RICO legislation in the abortion controversy. *Cf.* National Org. for Women v. Scheir, 114 S. Ct. 798 (1994). In addition, puzzling linedrawing issues involving partisan political activity are created by a decision involving the federal Mail Fraud Act. United States v. Margiotta, 688 F.2d 108 (2d Cir. 1982).

122. *E.g.,* A. Goldstein, *Conspiracy to Defraud the United States,* 68 YALE L.J. 405 (1959); Johnson, *The Unnecessary Crime of Conspiracy,* 61 CAL. L. REV. 1137 (1973); Marcus, *Criminal Conspiracy Law: Time to Turn Back from an Ever Expanding, Ever Troubling Area,* 1 WM. & MARY BILL RTS. J. 1 (1992).

123. United States v. Hernandez, 896 F.2d 513 (11th Cir. 1990), is illustrative. *See* discussion of the case in Marcus, *supra* note 122, at 20.

124. The best brief summary of the perils confronting the accused in a conspiracy prosecution remains the concurring opinion of Justice Robert Jackson in Krulewitch v. United States, 336 U.S. 440, 453 (1949).

125. The relaxation of the hearsay rule with reference to declarations of co-conspirators has evolved into an even more potent prosecutorial weapon in recent years. Professor Marcus has recently commented: "The line of Supreme Court decisions in the last decade has dramatically changed the practice in terms of hearsay evidence offered at conspiracy trials . . . . United States District Judge Thomas Flannery of the District of Columbia, himself a former United States Attorney, stated the matter well. 'The prosecutor has an easy task in introducing damaging evidence against co-conspirators because of the relaxed rules in conspiracy cases.'" *Supra* note 122, at 32.

126. *Cf.* comment of Judge Marvin Aspen in United States v. Andrews, 754 F. Supp. 1161, 1176 (N.D. Ill. 1990): "It is fanciful to believe that any jury would be able, or even willing, to intelligently and thoroughly deliberate over the enormous volume of evidence expected in a single trial of this action. In its present form, the trial would involve twenty-two to twenty-nine defendants accused of over 150 factually separate criminal acts spanning a period of over twenty years and involving at least twenty-five different provisions of state and federal penal codes."

127. "While it is certainly true that in 1952, and even in 1972, one would have an easy time finding conspiracy prosecutions in all jurisdictions in the United States, what we see today is nothing short of a miracle in terms of the number of conspiracy prosecutions . . . . Much of this increase is directly attributable to the sharp increase in drug prosecutions which most often involve conspiracy charges." Marcus, *supra* note 122, at 8.

128. For further comment of the effect of the RICO statute on the conspiracy device, see Bradley, *supra* note 97, at 878; Halderman, *Reconsidering RICO's Conspiracy and "Group" Enterprise Concepts with Traditional Conspiracy Doctrine*, 52 U. CIN. L. REV. 385 (1983); Marcus, *supra* note 122, at 43; Comment, Eliott v. United States: *Conspiracy Law and the Judicial Pursuit of Organized Crime Through RICO*, 65 VA. L. REV. 109 (1978).

129. Racketeer Influenced & Corrupt Organizations Act, Pub. L. No. 91–452, tit. IX, 84 Stat. 941–47 (1970), *codified as amended at* 18 U.S.C. §§ 1961–1968 (1988).

130. Mail Fraud Act, ch. 321. 35 Stat. 1130 (codified as amended at 18 U.S.C. §§ 1341, 1342 (1988)); Wire Fraud Act, ch. 879, 66 Stat. 722, (codified as amended at 18 U.S.C. § 1343 (1988)).

131. Blakey & Gettings, *Racketeer Influenced and Corrupt Organizations (RICO): Basic Concepts and Civil Remedies*, 53 TEMP. L.Q. 1009 (1980); McClellan, *The Organized Crime Act (S.30) or Its Critics: Which Threatens Civil Liberties?*, 46 NOTRE DAME LAW. 55 (1970).

132. *E.g.*, United States v. Mandel, 591 F.2d 1347 (4th Cir. 1979); United States v. States, 488 F.2d 761 (8th Cir. 1973).

133. This view appears to be that of a majority of the Supreme Court in McNally v. United States, 483 U.S. 350 (1987); *see also* Comment, *The Intangible-Rights Doctrine and Political Corruption Prosecutions Under the Federal Mail Fraud Statute*, 47 U. CHI. L. REV. 562 (1980).

134. Thus, very early the statute was interpreted to apply to cases of "promissory fraud," contrary to prevailing definitions of the crime of false pretenses. Durland v. United States, 161 U.S. 306 (1896). Subsequent holdings have extended the Act to reckless, as well as false, promises. United States v. Edwards, 458 F.2d 875, 881 (5th Cir. 1972).

135. *Cf.* United States v. Brown, 540 F.2d 364 (8th Cir. 1976); United States v. Isaacs, 493 F.2d 1124 (7th Cir. 1974); United States v. McNeive, 536 F.2d 1245 (8th Cir. 1976).

136. Bronston v. United States, 658 F.2d 920 (2d Cir. 1981); *see* Coffee, *From Tort to Crime: Some Reflections on the Criminaliza-*

tion of Fiduciary Breaches and the Problematic Line Between Law and Ethics, 19 AM. CRIM. L. REV. 117, 130 (1981).

137. United States v. Margiotta, 688 F.2d 108 (2d Cir. 1982). Judge Kaufman for the court remarked: "The drawing of standards in this area is a most difficult enterprise." *Id.* at 122.

138. United States v. Mandel, 591 F.2d 1347, 1361 (4th Cir. 1979). In McNally v. United States, 483 U.S. 350 (1987), the Supreme Court finally rejected the "intangible rights" readings of the Mail Fraud Act and confined the concept of fraud to behavior aimed at pecuniary and property gain. The following year, however, Congress introduced a little-noticed provision into the voluminous Anti-Drug Abuse Act (18 U.S.C. § 1346 (1988)), having as its apparent purpose the resurrection of the "intangible rights" theory rejected in the *McNally* case.

139. "[W]hat profoundly troubles me is the potential for abuse through selective prosecution and the degree of raw political power the freeswinging club of mail fraud affords federal prosecutors." United States v. Margiotta, 688 F.2d 108, 143 (2d Cir. 1982) (Winter, J., dissenting).

140. "Congress viewed RICO principally as a tool for attacking the specific problem of infiltration of legitimate business by organized criminal syndicates. As such, RICO has hardly been a dramatic success. Few notable RICO prosecutions have dealt directly with this sort of criminal activity." Lynch, *RICO: The Crime of Being a Criminal* (pts. 1 & 2), 87 COLUM. L. REV. 661, 662 (1987).

141. 18 U.S.C. § 1962 (a)–(d) (1988).

142. *Id.* § 1961(5): "'[P]attern of racketeering activity' requires at least two acts of racketeering activity, one of which occurred after the effective date of this chapter and the last of which occurred within ten years (excluding any period of imprisonment) after the commission of a prior act of racketeering activity."

143. *Id.* § 1961(1).

144. *E.g.,* FLA. STAT. § 895.02 (1990); *see* Dowd, *Interpreting RICO: In Florida, the Rules Are Different,* 40 U. FLA. L. REV. 127, 136 (1988) ("The breadth of the federal definition of 'racketeering activity' pales in comparison with the Florida definition.").

145. 492 U.S. 229 (1989).

146. *Id.* at 237.

147. *Id.* at 238.

148. *Compare* Roeder v. Alpha Indus., Inc., 814 F.2d 22 (1st Cir. 1987) *with* Superior Oil Co. v. Fulmer, 785 F.2d 252 (8th Cir. 1986).

149. 492 U.S. at 243.

150. *See supra* note 121.

151. Speaking of judicial developments in the application of the mail fraud legislation, Judge Ralph K. Winter, in dissent, remarked: "However logical this growth of the law may seem, it leads to a result which is not only greater than, but is roughly the square of, the sum of the parts. The proposition that any person active in political affairs who fails to disclose a fact material to that participation to the public is guilty of mail fraud finds not the slightest basis in Congressional intent, statutory language, or common canons of statutory interpretation." United States v. Margiotta, 688 F.2d 108, 142 (2d Cir. 1982). *See also* United States v. Mandel, 414 F. Supp. 997, 1021 (D. Md. 1976), *reversed en banc,* 602 F.2d 653 (4th Cir. 1979).

152. *E.g.,* United States v. Turkette, 452 U.S. 676 (1981) (involving definition of "enterprise" in RICO statute, 18 U.S.C. § 1961(4) (1988)). For commentary, *see* Allen, *A Crisis of Legality in the Criminal Law?,* 42 MER. L. REV. 811, 835–36 (1991) ("[T]he consequence, again, is a serious and continuing obscurity in the scope of the statute."); Lynch, *supra* note 140, at 701.

153. *Cf.* ATIYAH & SUMMERS, *supra* note 91, at 308.

154. STANDARDS OF AMERICAN LEGISLATION 288 (1917, 1965).

155. Margiotta v. United States, 688 F.2d 108, 120 (2d Cir. 1982).

156. On the various issues presented, consult Zimring, *The Multiple Middle Grounds Between Civil and Criminal Law,* 101 YALE L.J. 1901 (1992).

157. For a discussion by a critic of these developments, *see* Lowie, *The Welfare State, the New Regulation, and the Rule of Law, in* THE RULE OF LAW: IDEAL OR IDEOLOGY 17 (Hutchinson & Monahan eds. 1987).

158. Pub. L. No. 91–596, 84 Stat. 1590 (codified as amended in scattered sections of 5, 15, 18, 29, 42, 49 U.S.C.).

159. 29 U.S.C. § 651 (1970).

160. *Id.* § 655.

161. What is suggested is not akin to Jeremy Bentham's dream of a ministry of justice with comprehensive powers of law reform and codification, a vision, while never coming to fruition, has nevertheless proved influential in British law reform efforts to the present. Nor is the suggestion that of creating independent law reform commissions of the sort that have forwarded legislation to Parliament since 1965 and that have provided useful impetus to statutory reform throughout the world, including several American states. *See* W. HURLBURT, LAW REFORM COMMISSIONS IN THE UNITED KINGDOM, AUSTRALIA, AND CANADA (1986). What is most needed in Congress, which, unlike the British Parliament, pos-

sesses only a limited scope of legislative authority, is perhaps less an agency for proposing new ventures of law reform than an internal mechanism for auditing the record of legislation already enacted. In many areas of important public concern, the committee system has proved inadequate to provide such information vital to developing coherent and effective legislative policy. How have statutes in the field been read by courts, and are those understandings compatible with legislative purposes? Have the federal judicial circuits arrived at conflicting interpretations, thereby depriving the country of uniformity in important areas of penal legislation, and can the conflicts be resolved more quickly and surely by amendatory legislation than by the uncertain interventions of the Supreme Court on certiorari? Has the experience with statutes in the courts revealed problems and considerations that could not have been contemplated when the legislation was enacted? These and many more inquiries could constitute parts of the legislative audit.

Chapter 4. Summation

1. Allen, *Majorities, Minorities, and Morals: Penal Policy and Consensual Behavior,* 9 NN. KY. L. REV. 1, 17 *et seq.* (1982).

2. *See* S. ELLMANN, IN A TIME OF TROUBLE: LAW AND LIBERTY IN SOUTH AFRICA'S STATE OF EMERGENCY 44 *et seq.* (1992).

Index

impact of modern crime policy
on, 38, 39, 40–42, 47
implications of discretion for,
25–26
importance of adjudication to,
18
importance of spirit and tradition of, 6–7
importance to criminal justice,
5–6
independent judiciary, 18
institutional habits as a measure of vitality, 6–7, 94
institutional structure limits,
57–63
interpretation and application of
law as legality issues, 17–18
legality not the exclusive social
virtue, 96
magistrates as threats to, 77
mail fraud legislation as a
threat to, 87–88
in medieval thought, 3–4
normative values of formal legality, 22
not only device to limit official
power, 19–20
nulla poena a central concept,
14
opposed to arbitrary power, 14
origin of phrase, 3
persistence of legal forms, 97
public understanding and support for, 98
and realist jurisprudence, 9–10
responsibility of the legally
trained, 99
as restraint on public officials, 4
as a revolutionary idea, 4
RICO as a threat to, 88–89
rules as the central device, 20
statutory interpretation as a
threat to, 77–83
vital to liberal societies, 14, 94
See also Drug-law enforcement;
Nulla poena sine lege; Realist
jurisprudence; Rules, legal;
"War on crime"

Rules, legal
causes of normlessness, 24–25
central legality device, 20
failure to achieve rules as basic
pathology, 20
failures to achieve in substantive law, 21–22
individualized justice as a
source of skepticism, 21–22
ineptness of as a source of
skepticism, 21
language skepticism produces
rule skepticism, 21
normlessness of American criminal justice, 24, 73, 77
objects of modern skepticism
and hostility, 20–21
some functions not amenable
to, 24–25, 63
varied forms of enforcement, 20

Sentencing guidelines, federal
alleged absurdities of, 75–76
arbitrary potential of unregulated sentencing, 74
balance of rule and individualized justice, 76–77
content influenced by "war on
crime," 75
difficulties reflect value conflicts, 76–77
federal and state legislation, 74
illustrate difficulties of reform,
73–74
influence on adversary process,
34
neglect of offender characteristics and situational factors,
75
neglect of proportionality principle, 43–44
reduced role of probation, 75
sentencing disparities, 74–75
state experience as a basis of
reform, 77
Sentencing Reform Act of 1984,
74
Single-issue politics, 95